China under Communism

D0034142

Despite the demise of communism throughout the world, a quarter of the world's population still remains firmly under the Communist banner. *China under Communism* examines the history of the Chinese communists since their accession to power in 1949, through the tumult of ongoing revolution under Mao to the new era of economic reforms and the handover of Hong Kong.

Alan Lawrance examines the problems facing the Communists at home and abroad in 1949 and assesses the initial successes of the new regime. He shows how Mao's brand of Marxism was eventually replaced by pragmatic policies. He includes discussion of:

* changing relationships with the Soviet Union and the USA
* the Great Leap Forward and the Cultural Revolution
* the rise of market forces under Deng Xiaoping, leading to impressive economic growth
* problems of modernization, and the crushing of demand for political reform in Tiananmen Square

With comprehensive endnotes drawing attention to further reading and historiographical debate, *China under Communism* is an invaluable concise introduction to China from 1949 to the present day.

Alan Lawrance is Visiting Research Fellow at the University of Hertfordshire.

The Making of the Contemporary World
Edited by Eric Evans and Ruth Henig
University of Lancaster

The Making of the Contemporary World series provides challenging interpretations of contemporary issues and debates within strongly defined historical frameworks. The range of the series is global, with each volume drawing together material from a range of disciplines – including economics, politics and sociology. The books in this series present compact, indispensable introductions for students studying the modern world.

China under Communism

Alan Lawrance

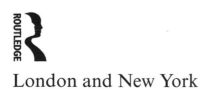

London and New York

First published 1998 by Routledge
11 New Fetter Lane, London EC4P 4EE

Simultaneously published in the USA and Canada
by Routledge
29 West 35th Street, New York, NY 10001

© 1998 Alan Lawrance

Typeset in Times by M Rules
Printed and bound in Great Britain by
T J International Ltd, Padstow, Cornwall

British Library Cataloguing in Publication Data
A catalogue record for this book is available from the British Library

Library of Congress Cataloging in Publication Data
Lawrance, Alan, 1930–
    China under communism / Alan Lawrance
    p.   cm.   —(The making of the contemporary world)
    Includes bibliographical references and index.
    1. China—History—1949– Chronology. 2. China—Foreign
    relations—1949– 3. China—Politics and government—1949–
    I. Title. II. Series.
    DS777.55.L384   1998
    951.05—dc21   98–17286
                                                                  CIP

ISBN 0–415–18692–7 (hbk)
ISBN 0–415–15045–0 (pbk)

Contents

Illustrations

Preface

When the writer first went to China in 1972, the chairman of the reception committee in Shanghai said, 'you have come from a far corner of the world and we welcome you.' Thus he was upholding the traditional view of China (Zhongguo), literally the 'middle kingdom', the centre of the world as it is depicted on Chinese maps.

The inscrutable 'middle kingdom' has featured in many Western views of China. If some early visitors reacted to the less easily penetrable aspects of Chinese civilization with amusement or contempt, others have marvelled at the special qualities. This perceived distinctiveness of China was compounded when the Communists took over, operating in seclusion behind a 'bamboo curtain'. How can we explain the excitement, the irrationality and sometimes both which have characterized the process of getting to know China. To take two examples: how could an American secretary of state, Dean Acheson, misinterpreting China's past, announce in 1949 that 'ultimately . . . the democratic individualism of China' would reassert itself? Why did Henry Kissinger, as he stepped forward to shake hands with a totteringly frail old man – Chairman Mao – feel that never before had he been in the presence of someone 'who so distilled raw concentrated willpower'?[1]

Does the element of strangeness in the image of China impede real understanding? Certainly Westerners have been faced with variously distorted impressions in addition to the obviously hostile propaganda of the Cold War and the unquestioning adoration of everything Red and Chinese by some western (left-wing) visitors.[2]

While serious historical scholarship has avoided such pitfalls, it has not been entirely free of the influence and uncertainties of the Cold War period and some historical controversy has reflected political attitudes. Moreover, work on China has been constrained by a lack of reliable materials.

From 1949 on the 'China Watchers', based largely in Hong Kong and well-funded by the USA, had limited access, speculating largely from official publications and rumours. The first flood of new and controversial material became available as a result of the Cultural Revolution in the 1960s when the so-called Red Guard publications found their way out via Hong Kong. Then after Mao's death in 1976 and with the opening-up in the late 1970s and 1980s new materials became available. With glasnost, materials in the Soviet Union were released which shed some new light on China. Some of the earlier writings on Communist China were found to be oversimplified if not inaccurate. Much more is known about Mao, his relationship with his colleagues and the Soviet leaders and, for example, his decision to intervene in the Korean War. In China the official view no longer precludes contributions by specialist historians.

During the last fifty years there have been dramatic and unforeseen shifts in the course of China's history. Who would have foreseen in 1947 that by 1949 the communists would rule all China? In 1949 could anyone have envisaged the massive experiment of the Great Leap Forward and its failure by 1959? In 1950, when the Sino-Soviet treaty was signed, who had the foresight to predict an irreconcilable Sino-Soviet rift by the 1960s? When Mao was sidelined in 1959 who imagined that within ten years he would become the most idolized figure in the whole of Chinese history, his ideas, however bizarre, apparently accepted without question. Was it conceivable in the early 1970s that within a decade socialism would be on the way out? And who but the most optimistic would have predicted a 10 per cent annual growth rate throughout the 1980s?

This book provides a concise history of China since 1949 within a chronological framework. It introduces the reader to main areas of historical controversy and includes recent interpretations based on newly available material. Particular attention has been given to foreign relations, commensurate both with the theme of China as an emerging world power and with the need to set China in context for students of the contemporary world. It has been possible to take the story to the end of 1997 – a significant year for China. In February Deng Xiaoping, arguably the last of the emperor-style rulers, died. On 1 July Hong Kong was handed over complete with its system of capitalism, law and democracy, which could yet survive and even prosper as an alternative to communist totalitarianism, and in September the Fifteenth Party Congress made policy and leadership decisions which will affect China well into the twenty-first century.

Acknowledgements

Very many thanks are due to those who have helped and encouraged me in the preparation of this book. For their expert criticism I am particularly indebted to Professor Hua Qingzhao of the Tianjin Academy of Social Sciences, Sybille van der Sprenkel, formerly of the Sociology Department at Leeds University and Professor Wilson Hoffman of Hiram College, USA. Paul Wingrove of the University of Greenwich helped to bring me up to date following his recent researches in Moscow. Needless to say I am entirely responsible for the opinions expressed and any remaining errors. For general advice, checking details and proof-reading I am indebted to Loretto Lynch, Ben Perks, Christina Reedyk and Jo Walley. Of many helpful librarians I must thank in particular Neil Allen at the University of Hertfordshire and Laura Rifkin of the SACU Library at the GB–China Centre. Thanks also to Fuchsia Dunlop for the loan of the postage stamp celebrating Sino–Soviet friendship in 1950. Ruth Grillo has done a masterly job processing the text with unfailing good humour. Throughout, April Carter's advice and encouragement has been indispensable.

Chronology

CHINA			FOREIGN RELATIONS	
1949	*1 Oct.*	PRC proclaimed		
1950	*June*	Land Reform Law	*Feb.*	Sino-Soviet Treaty
	Oct.	Troops sent to Tibet	*Oct.*	Chinese volunteers enter Korea
1953	*Jan.*	Five Year Plan projected	*Mar.*	Death of Stalin
			July	Korean Armistice
1954	*Sept.*	NPC adopts constitution	*April–July*	Geneva Conference
1956	*May*	Mao's '100 flowers' speech	*Feb.*	Khrushchev denounces Stalin
1957	*Summer*	'100 flowers' at height	*Oct.*	USSR launches Sputnik
			Nov.	Mao's 'East wind prevails' speech
1958		Great Leap Forward. Communes	*31 July*	Khrushchev arrives in Beijing
			Aug.–Oct.	Shelling of Jinmen (Quemoy)
1959		Lin Biao replaces Peng Dehuai	*Sept.*	Khrushchev visits US, quarrels with Mao
1960		Economic problems compounded by natural disasters		USSR withdraws experts
1962	*Sept.*	Socialist Education Movement	*Oct.*	Cuban Crisis. Sino-Indian War
1964	*Oct.*	China tests atom bomb	*Aug.*	China denounces US involvement in Vietnam

CHINA			FOREIGN RELATIONS	
1966		Cultural Revolution launched		
1968	*Sept.*	Revolutionary Committees restore order	*Aug.*	China denounces invasion of Czechoslovakia
1969	*April*	Ninth Party Congress	*Mar.*	Clashes with USSR on Ussuri River
1971	*Sept.*	Lin Biao dies	*July*	Kissinger arranges Nixon visit (1972)
			Oct.	PRC replaces Taiwan regime at UN
1972			*Feb.*	President Nixon in China, signs Shanghai Communiqué
1976	*Jan.*	Zhou Enlai dies		
	April	Tiananmen demonstration		
	Sept.	Mao Zedong dies		
	Oct.	Hua Guofeng becomes Chairman		
1978	*Dec.*	Coca-Cola gets China franchise	*Aug.*	Sino-Japanese Peace Treaty
	Dec.	Democracy Wall movement		
1979	*Mar.*	Wei Jingsheng arrested	*Jan.*	Deng Xiaoping in US cements Sino-US relations
		Clamp down on Democracy Wall	*Feb.*	China–Vietnam War
	April	Proposal to set up Special Economic Zones		
1979–85		Family responsibility system introduced		China in IMF and World Bank
1980		Deng's protégés, Hu Yaobang and Zhao Ziyang, promoted		
1984		Economic reform extended in urban sector	*Sept.*	Sino-British agreement on Hong Kong handover
1986		Calls for political reform		

CHINA		FOREIGN RELATIONS	
1987	Hu Yaobang dismissed		
1989 *April*	Tiananmen protest starts, leading to crackdown in June	*May*	Gorbachev's visit to Beijing
1991			Break-up of Soviet Union
1992 *Jan.–Feb.*	Deng Xiaoping tours south China promoting drive for modernization		
1997 *Feb.*	Deng Xiaoping dies	*April*	Jiang Zemin visits Moscow: 'New bilateral relationship'
Sept.	Fifteenth Party Congress	*June*	Handover of Hong Kong
1998 *March*	Premier Li Peng retires after statutory maximum two terms and is succeeded by Zhu Rongji	*June*	President Clinton visits China

Abbreviations

APC	Agricultural Producers' Co-operative
CC	Central Committee
CCP	Chinese Communist Party
CPPCC	Chinese People's Political Consultative Conference
CPSU	Communist Party of the Soviet Union
DPRK	Democratic People's Republic of Korea (North Korea)
DRV	Democratic Republic of Vietnam (North Vietnam)
GMD	Guomindang (Kuomintang)
NPC	National People's Congress
PLA	People's Liberation Army
PRC	People's Republic of China
ROC	Republic of China (Taiwan)
SALT	Strategic Arms Limitation Talks
SEATO	South-east Asian Treaty Organization

Romanization
Chinese names are given in pinyin with the exception of a few well known people and places such as Chiang Kai-shek, Sun Yat-sen, Hong Kong and Tibet which are given in their familiar form.

Map of People's Republic of China

Introduction

'I have predicted that full-scale capitalist restoration may appear in China. I think it will be bad then.' So Mao Zedong is reported to have said in June 1976 at a last meeting with a group of Party colleagues.[1] The very old man did not elaborate. Was it said as a warning or with a resigned sigh? After leading the Chinese Communists with apparently unshaken conviction for 55 years, Mao uttered a doubt which was to portend the end of socialism in China.

Within a decade of Mao's death the capitalist objectives at the end of the 'revisionist road' had become clear. 'To get rich is glorious' is a long way from 'To rebel is justified': it is a tribute of some sort to the resilience of the Chinese Communist Party.

The First Party Congress of thirteen men in a boat on a lake in Shanghai in 1921 included the man who in 1949 proclaimed the People's Republic in Tiananmen Square. For Mao Zedong twenty-eight years of revolutionary struggle were followed by twenty-seven years of mixed achievements presiding over what was the largest, and arguably the most devout, Marxist regime.

A significant period for one man in politics is not a long time in the three thousand years history of China's civilization. In fact the rise and fall of the Communist dynasty may well be encompassed in less than one century – only the terminal date remains to be entered. Historians have to explain how a Marxist regime took root and flourished in such an unlikely setting; how the traditional culture, mores and trading instincts of so many were apparently subordinated to the ideals of so few at the top of the superstructure.

One explanation is found in the nature of traditional Confucianism, which stressed order and stability in a hierarchical structure, extending theoretically from family up through officialdom to the Emperor, the son of Heaven, who was responsible for maintaining the system, hence the duty of obedience to seniors.[2] Certainly the traditions of

Confucianism put stress on social harmony, stability, hierarchy and rule by the wise. But it does not follow that this tradition contributed significantly to the rise of the CCP. Historians who reject a culturally based explanation say that the communists succeeded because they offered honest government and stability after years of corruption and turmoil. Moreover, they emerged as the patriots who stood up to the Japanese and eventually unified the country.

It is not in the scope of this book to cover the Communists' rise to power, but a summary of their achievements before 1949 is a necessary background to understanding what happened when at last they came into the cities and set about conducting the great experiment which has proved to be so temporary.

THE EMERGENCE OF THE CHINESE COMMUNISTS

Chinese Communists frequently referred to foreign imperialism and 'feudalism' as the twin evils of the old regime. The imperialists were the nineteenth-century invaders led by the British who by bombardment forced the Qing dynasty, already on the decline, to open its doors to Western trade, to cede Hong Kong and allow Westerners to set up autonomous enclaves in the 'treaty ports'.

The Chinese empire was the oldest continuing civilization; it covered an area larger than the continental United States and its population accounted for a quarter of mankind. After their earlier technological achievements[3] the Chinese had failed to keep pace with the western scientific revolution which, through technology, produced both demand for expanding markets and the military might to conquer the world. The Qing dynasty were the heirs to the once magnificent and self-sufficient 'Middle Kingdom'. However, they were handicapped not only by the lack of technology but by 'feudalism'. This term embraced almost everything backward in society – an outmoded administrative system and a hierarchy of rich and poor, landlord and tenant. As the Communists saw it, the Chinese repressed by feudalism were subject to the rapacious incursion of western imperialism.

Since the nineteenth century Chinese reformers had debated how far and for what purpose Western knowledge should be accepted. It was argued that Western learning was for use; Chinese learning remained the essence. Thus in its later years the Qing had accepted the need for reforms while hoping to preserve the underlying Confucian ethics and had taken some steps on the road to modernization with the reform of education, the army and even administration. But the process of reform had been unable to prevent the fall of the dynasty by early 1912.

The republican reformers under Sun Yat-sen were prepared for more fundamental social change but Sun, who had a penchant for western ways especially political democracy, lacked the ability and the resources to put his ideals into practice. His 1911 revolution gave way almost immediately to the military leader Yuan Shikai who had little time for political assemblies.

When Yuan died in 1915, having tried and failed to make himself Emperor, power fell into the hands of regional warlords, holding sway in their own provinces while Westerners continued to profit in territorial enclaves.[4] The Chinese resented their perceived inferiority. The oft-quoted sign in a Shanghai park – 'No Admission to Dogs and Chinese' probably never existed[5] but the Chinese felt with reason that they were being treated like dogs.

When China's legitimate claims at the Versailles Peace Conference were overridden in favour of Japan, student protests on 4 May 1919 sparked off an intellectual reform movement which was ready to reject rather than modify old ideas. This date was a turning point which marks the beginning of a new period in Chinese history. In 1919 those who joined the mounting demand for effective change were faced with two contrasting routes to reform: modernization based on American and British models and the Marxist-Leninist way exemplified in the recent Russian revolution.

Sun Yat-sen and his followers in the Nationalist Party (Guomindang) favoured the former but they were prepared to co-operate with emissaries sent by the Soviets. In 1924 when Sun Yat-sen met Adolph Joffe in Shanghai it was agreed that China's 'most pressing problem is to achieve national unification and attain full national independence'.[6] Therefore the Guomindang would accept help from Russia. This arrangement was sweetened by Soviet Russia offering to renounce 'all the treaties and exactions which the Tsardom imposed on China'.

Some members of Sun's Nationalist party (the GMD) went to Moscow for training while military advisers, e.g. Galen, were attached to Sun's staff. This had the effect of giving the GMD a Leninist structure. When Sun died in 1925 it was the military leader Chiang Kai-shek who replaced him.

Already Comintern agent Maring had been sent to help organize the small separate Communist party groups into a national party. Mao Zedong was one of the delegates to the First Party Congress in 1921, which in order to avoid the police, conducted most of its business in a boat on a Shanghai lake. In 1923 under pressure from the Russians the

Communists became card carrying members of the GMD in a united front. This early alliance was shattered in 1927 when Chiang Kai-shek, having led a northern expedition from Guangzhou to Shanghai instigated a massacre there of his left-wing supporters. Some Communists who escaped went underground in the cities; others organized resistance in the countryside and remote mountain districts.

Mao Zedong already had some experience of working with the peasantry. His first major written work was a *Report on the Peasant Movement in Hunan* published in 1927 a month before the Shanghai coup. After an abortive attempt to take over the city of Nanchang some of the Communists took to the mountains bordering the provinces of Jiangxi and Hunan. Remote from comrades in the cities who were being exhorted by Moscow to carry out urban insurrection, Mao, who was out of favour with the Chinese Politburo, collaborated with Zhu De, the military commander, in forming the first Red Army and Soviet in April 1928.

Meanwhile the Nationalist forces under Chiang Kai-shek had reached Beijing, brought the warlords into line and were setting out to unify China under a modern republican regime. There were two problems: the Japanese were about to take Manchuria and the Communists were establishing bases in central China. Chiang decided that his priority would be to defeat the latter, whom he saw as a 'disease of the heart' rather than the foreign invaders a 'disease of the skin'. Indeed it may well have been impossible for him to resist effectively the well-equipped Japanese army and airforce at that time. He did succeed after four years of military campaigning, with the aid of German officers, in overrunning the Soviet base in Jiangxi, but the Red Army escaped and in the epic year-long march in 1934–5 was able to join up with a small Communist base in the north-west province of Shaanxi. Less than a tenth of the marchers reached their destination but it was an augury of survival. Remote Yanan became the home of Communism in China (Yanan became the Communist capital in December 1936) and Mao Zedong, elected during the Long March, remained leader until he died. Chiang Kai-shek for all his apparent successes and despite enjoying the respect and sympathy of most of the world had appeared less than heroic in his failure to stand up to the Japanese. In a bizarre incident in December 1936 at Xian, Chiang's own officers took him prisoner and he was released on an understanding that the civil war should end.[7] This led to an agreement to form a second united front against the Japanese. The communist negotiator Zhou Enlai helped to set this up and the Soviets pressed Mao, who had reservations, to accept the arrangement.[8]

The agreement served the Communists well when in July 1937 the Japanese launched attacks which developed into the invasion of north and central China. Chiang Kai-shek only avoided outright defeat by retreating. The Communists with their well tried guerilla tactics harassed the Japanese behind the lines while extending their control over the country districts and co-operating patriotically with the peasantry. Sympathetic Western commentators[9] pictured Mao as a Robin Hood leading peasant volunteers by moral example in contrast with the bullying and corruption associated with Chiang Kai-shek.

THE IDEOLOGY OF CHINESE COMMUNISM

What was the nature of Chinese Communism as it developed up to 1949? In what ways was it distinct? What did it owe to Mao Zedong?

As Marx, Engels and Lenin have always been held up as exemplary revolutionaries by the Chinese Communists it might be supposed that the ideology of the CCP was closely akin to that of the Soviet Union. In fact Mao's own theories were distinctive. Although he had followed Marx in his commitment to class warfare, Mao saw the peasants rather than the workers as the vanguard of the revolution.

The important period for the formulation of Mao's ideas was at Yanan during the anti-Japanese War. At the communist headquarters behind the lines cadres on leave mixed with recent recruits who had travelled from all over the country to join the resistance movement. A system of training and indoctrination was necessary. This was the origin of the anti-Japanese military and political 'university' of Yanan, where especially during the rectification movement of 1941–4, education and ideology went hand in hand. For Mao it provided the occasion for confirming his position.[10] He brought rivals – including a group of Moscow trained communists – into conformity with his ideas.[11] He emerged clearly as both the intellectual and political leader. He showed the importance of applying the ideas of Marxism-Leninism to the actual conditions of China. Moreover, Mao emphasised the importance of testing ideas in practice. In contrast to the effete traditions of Chinese scholarship, which favoured long fingernails, Mao stressed the hands-on approach. 'If you want knowledge, you must take part in the process of changing reality. If you want to know the taste of a pear, you must change the pear by eating it yourself. There can be no knowledge apart from practice.' He castigated the 'know-alls' and the book learners. To Mao a professor of physics who could not repair the field radio was useless.

The Marxist concept of democratic centralism paid lip service to the ideal of party cadres listening to the needs of the masses. For Mao the mass-line was a necessary component of socialism. He had genuine respect for the practical experience of the people, particularly the peasants. 'From the masses to the masses' meant as Mao taught it that the young cadres, especially those intellectual idealists who had come from the cities, would do well to listen to the old men in the countryside.

'In the masses is embodied great socialist activism'[12] believed Mao. It was not solely impersonal economic forces which determined the course of history but the conscious will of men committed to revolution. Thus it was necessary for the leadership to draw out and develop the nationalist and revolutionary element in the Chinese spirit. Moreover, this 'correct ideological consciousness' had to be maintained. Individuals would require 'remoulding'. Two aphorisms on the methods used, 'Cure the sickness to save the patient', 'Criticism, unity, criticism' show the pressures to conform in which a campaign could become a purge.

Whereas Lenin writing in 1917 in *The State and Revolution* envisaged the withering away of the state, Mao advocated the intensification of state power for the time being. On the eve of the Communist takeover in 'On the People's Democratic Dictatorship' Mao did predict tersely that the state would eventually wither away. The working class, the labouring people and the Communist Party must 'work hard' to create the conditions in which classes, state power, and political parties will die out naturally and mankind will enter the realm of Great Harmony. It is significant that Mao used *Da Tong* (Great Harmony) a term dating from the fourth century BC, for the (eventual) goal of communism.[13]

Western academics have debated Mao's relation to Marxism. Some have queried whether he was a true Marxist, while others have argued that his thought was firmly rooted in Stalinism and added nothing really original to Marxism-Leninism.[14] In China, Mao's ideas were entitled 'Mao Zedong thought' – they were not dignified worldwide by the term Maoism before the Cultural Revolution.[15]

In 1949 Mao was stressing the need for the Communist Party to take the lead in making revolution. Since in China the united front, which had operated particularly to the Communists' advantage in the anti-Japanese war, was to be the keystone of post-liberation policy it was all the more necessary that the party should lead and organize the social classes in the new national context of a united 'liberated' China.

1 The Communist victory and consolidation of power, 1949–53

> *We shall soon put aside some of the things we know well and be compelled to do things we don't know well . . . We must learn to do economic work from all who know how, no matter who they are.*
>
> Mao Zedong, 30 June 1949.
> *'On the People's Democratic Dictatorship'.*

The inherent weaknesses of the Nationalist regime were a major reason for the Communist victory in the civil war. The unexpected collapse of the Nationalists in 1949 gave the CCP a mandate to govern the whole of China. Starting with very limited experience of ruling big cities and industrial areas they were remarkably successful. Within three years they had united the country, revived industry and communications and had begun to promote social revolution in a new political framework.

WHY THE NATIONALISTS LOST THE CIVIL WAR

It is a paradox that the Nationalists were unable to proceed to ultimate success despite their apparently advantageous position in 1945. They were the internationally recognized government of China supported diplomatically by both the United States and the Soviet Union.[1] They had a large army of which 39 divisions were trained and equipped by the Americans and they had a virtual monopoly of airpower. The Communist fighting experience had been in guerrilla warfare rather than in the stand-up battle of tactics of large armies using sophisticated weapons. In military terms the Communists had serious losses by mid-1947 when the Nationalists took control of southern Manchuria. For a time the Communists were even driven out of Yanan, although this was of little more than symbolic importance.

However, the Nationalists were failing even before the Civil War erupted in 1946. The Japanese invasion of China and the circumstances of World War II were very important factors leading to Communist victory. The GMD was unable to stand up to the Japanese and effective resistance was largely in the hands of the Communists working behind the Japanese lines. Moreover, the Japanese had driven the Nationalists out of their bases of political power in the lower Yangzi region. When at the end of World War II the Nationalists returned to take over from the Japanese, they brought exploitation and corruption which alienated even those urban groups who saw socialism as a menace.[2] In contrast, the Communists in the (relatively few) cities they controlled, won support, after some initial excessive confiscation in Manchuria, by effective controls which encouraged productivity and curtailed labour agitation.

The Nationalists' failure to stop runaway inflation convinced a great many people, particularly the erstwhile middle classes, that they had nothing more to lose. At least the Communists were offering a new broom reputedly capable of sweeping away corruption and giving some stability to the wartorn nation. As the Communist armies began to gain ground in 1948, the Nationalist forces became increasingly demoralised. Some units deserted, others defected to the Communists. Few people, certainly not the Communists themselves, seem to have anticipated the speed with which the half of the country south of the Yangzi fell to the Reds after April 1949.

How far did the Communists' own ideas and policies promote their success? The mobilization of guerrilla forces went hand in hand with land reform. In the period of the united front against Japan the Communists' moderate aims of reducing rents and interest to benefit the poorer people in the countryside were widely accepted. Even the rural elite whose income was reduced appreciated the efficiency with which dues were collected under new village governments.

In May 1946 the Communists introduced in the 'liberated areas' a more radical policy intended to transfer land ownership to the poorer peasants. This was designed to confirm the loyalty of the majority of the villagers to the Communists in the impending civil war. The 1947 Land Law abolished landowner rights and authorised village associations to redistribute the land. The goal of 'land to the tiller' was being realized in accordance with the Communists' views of a hierarchy of peasant classes. The poorer and middle class peasants were to benefit but how precisely were the lines to be drawn and policies implemented? The problems raised led to the Directive on Land Reform and Party Rectification Work in February 1948. This February directive recognized that the attack on the middle peasants had gone too far. In 1948 the Central Committee accepted that middle peasants could make up to 25 per cent of their income by 'exploitation' e.g. from hiring seasonal hands, rent and interest.

By 1949 it would be unsafe to characterize the process of liberation as a victory of the exploited classes. Far more pragmatically than Marxist theory might imply, the Communists won allegiance by leading the attack on the obvious grievances such as corruption, rack rents and hypertaxation. Most importantly their record contrasted with the Nationalists' failure to implement reforms.

Explanations for the Communist victory must weigh the importance of their economic line and social policies against their strong political organization and military successes. These are not of course mutually exclusive.

PROBLEMS FACING THE NEW LEADERS

Who were the men about to become the leaders of a united China? In May 1949 there were about 4 million members in the Chinese Communist Party out of a total population estimated at 540 million. Their leader Mao Zedong, 55 years old in 1949, had been in charge of the Party since 8 January 1935, at Zunyi on the Long March.

With Mao since 1928 had been the military commander, Zhu De, rightly credited with the early successes of the Red Army. He remained as commander in chief of the newly named People's Liberation Army after 1949, and continued to be widely respected if less prominent in affairs.

Zhou Enlai, who went to Europe in 1920 with other revolutionary minded young Chinese in the aftermath of the 4 May Movement, became a leading negotiator for the Communists. During the anti-Japanese war he was in charge of the liaison with the Nationalists in Chongqing. From the time of the Long March he appears as a close supporter of Mao's policies. In 1949 he became Premier, the head of the state executive apparatus, and throughout his career also played a particularly important role in foreign affairs.

In 1949 the Party's second in command was Liu Shaoqi. During the Yanan years he strongly supported Mao's leadership and his political ideas. He had a leading role in the Chinese People's Political Consultative Conference which founded the People's Republic. Among other important posts he was the head of the labour federation and the Sino-Soviet Friendship Association. When Mao went to Moscow at the end of 1949, Liu took over state and party affairs as his deputy. He was widely regarded as Mao's successor (until 1966). Another supporter of Mao in his rise to power at Yanan was Chen Yun. Chen had a particular interest in economics and he was to hold a key position in the new republic as head of the Finance and Economic Commission directing measures for immediate economic rehabilitation and later helping to establish the Five Year Plan.

Peng Dehuai had joined Mao in the mountains in 1928. As military leader he rose to a position second only to Zhu De. Having directed the conquest of the north-west in the civil war he took charge of the administration of the North-west region. In 1950 he led the Chinese forces in Korea.

The problems facing the men who suddenly found themselves controlling the world's most populous country were daunting. They needed to eliminate their enemies, install their new government throughout the country and restore production, while taking steps towards modernizing backward areas of the economy.

The first was relatively straightforward. As Chiang Kai-shek fled desperately through parts of south and west China before heading for Taiwan, the majority of China's long-suffering people seemed prepared to accept the new regime. Mopping-up operations in Hainan, which fell to the Communists in April 1950, were extended to Xinjiang where various local independent regimes had to be suppressed. In October 1950 the Communist troops advanced into Tibet.

Lacking amphibian forces it was not easy to pursue Chiang and liberate Taiwan. In the case of the smaller islands, Zhoushan (Chusan) at the mouth of the Yangzi fell to the Communists in May 1950 while Jinmen (Quemoy) and Mazu (Matzu) a few miles off- shore remained in Nationalist hands.

The importance of the People's Liberation army in the new state was implicit in the division of the country into six regions.[3] Although these regions were geographically larger they were not unlike the macro-regions of the mid-Qing in that regional leaders held both military and administrative power over and above provincial governors.[4] The 1949 military regions were: North-east, North-west, North, East, Central–South and South-west. In each region there were four main posts: first party secretary, chairman of the military–political council (regional government), military commander and army political commissar. These twenty-four positions were held by a total of thirteen men since it was usual to hold more than one post.[5] The five most powerful men in this set-up were Gao Gang who held all four posts in the North-east – formerly Manchuria, Peng Dehuai who was both chairman and military commander in the North-west; Rao Shushi who held three posts in the East; Lin Biao who had three posts in the Central–South and Deng Xiaoping with two posts in the South-west. It may be noted that all five men sooner or later fell out with Mao Zedong and were purged.

Although they had ruled successfully in the base areas, the Communists lacked experience of city administration and they were inevitably dependent on the knowledge and expertise of administrators, traders and industrialists, few of whom were at that time inclined to communism or socialism. So in the summer of 1949 the CCP accepted a framework for a broad based society. Workers, peasants, petite bourgeoisie and national bourgeoisie were to have a recognized place in the new republic albeit under the leadership of the Communist party.[6] If it was not clear how long the status of all four classes would be preserved, they had the immediate satisfaction of being represented as four small stars alongside the large star of the Party on the new national flag.

The Communists, notwithstanding their long years in the country-side, recognized the need to introduce modern techniques if the economy were to thrive. It fitted the concept that China had been held back by 'feudal' oppression and foreign imperialists to assume that lib-eration would go hand in hand with economic growth. Overall China's economy had suffered during twelve years of war. In 1949 industrial production was half the pre-war level. Moreover, half of the 18,000 kilometres of railway track had been put out of action by military operations. On top of this something had to be done to restore a national currency after the disastrously high inflation of the GMD regime. Where would China find the necessary expertise and financial backing to promote modernization? Where at the least could China find trading partners?

It became clear in 1949 that the United States despite its past sym-pathy for China was not about to help the Communist regime. The publication of the *China White Paper*, in August 1949, explained the 'loss' of China to Communism, and those in the State Department who might be thought to have had any truck with the Chinese Reds were particularly concerned to save their careers now that China was on the wrong side in the Cold War.

THE NEW GOVERNMENT IN 1949

When Mao proclaimed the inauguration of the People's Republic on 1 October 1949 he highlighted the emergence of a new and independent

China. It was in the spirit of appealing to national unity that the Chinese People's Political Consultative Conference passed a temporary constitution (Organic Law) and set out policies (Common Programme) appropriate to a broad coalition. Eight 'democratic parties' were permitted, including the Guomindang Revolutionary Committee (comprised of former Nationalists), but the activities of these parties were controlled. The Communist Party directed the media which were bound to disseminate the Party line and promote the ideology of reform.

The idea of power sharing was exemplified in the ruling councils. The Government council chaired by Mao Zedong had six deputy chairpersons: three from the Communist Party, Liu Shaoqi, Zhu De and Gao Gang; plus Madame Sun Yat-sen (widow of the founder of the Republic of China), Li Jishen from the GMD Revolutionary Committee and Zhang Lan of the Democratic League. The State Administration Council (the cabinet) under Zhou Enlai had ten party members and eleven non-party members.

Government direction of the economy was facilitated by the degree of state control which had already been put in place by the Nationalist regime. The GMD had gone some way to taking over private assets, e.g. 90 per cent of the metallurgical industries, 73 per cent of machine building and 75 per cent of chemicals.[7] This process had been compounded by taking over all Japanese held property at the end of the World War in 1945. The new government's policy was to allow the private sector of industry and trade to continue for the time being. Businessmen were given some assurances in 1949 that the takeover of private enterprise was not imminent. Some entrepreneurs had preferred to flee to Hong Kong, Taiwan and elsewhere throughout the world. Although this was a loss of capital and expertise, it was offset by removing people potentially hostile to the new regime. But many industrialists and professional people remained to serve their homeland. A high proportion of scientists as well as writers and artists chose to stay.

COMMUNIST POLICIES, 1949–53

Within three years the new government had an impressive record of achievements. By the end of 1952 the gross output of industry and agriculture had risen by 77.5 per cent, back to pre-war levels. Coal production was up to 63.5 million tons, steel to 1.3 million tons, while grain production was ten per cent up on that of 1936, the best pre-war year. The railway system had been restored and expanded to 24,000 kilometres of track. Inflation was brought down; the new *renminbi* (people's currency) under tight control began to gain respect as one of the most stable currencies in the world.

Land reform in a relatively moderate form was to be extended across the whole country. The intention was to eliminate the landlords as a class and to redistribute land without destroying the middle peasants. There were important regional differences. In the provinces of the lower Yangzi farming was commercialized to an extent which benefited the wealthier peasants. It was realized that interference with the marketing of the agricultural surplus would be bad for the overall economy. This was taken into account in the Land Reform Law of 28 June 1950 which allowed rich peasants throughout China to retain, in addition to land worked by their families, land worked by hired hands and land rented out, provided it was no more than 50 per cent of the whole.

In the period 1947–52 land reform spreading across China during and after the civil war is calculated to have taken 40 per cent of China's arable land from 4 per cent of the people and redistributed it to 300 million peasants. Similarly tools, draught animals and housing were redistributed. The former landlords were denounced at 'speak bitterness' meetings. Many years ago Mao had said that 'a revolution is not a dinner party' and certainly the process of land reform had an element of violence which varied according to time and place and the zeal of local cadres. Landlords were also targets of the movement to suppress counter-revolutionaries which gained momentum from October 1950 when China entered the Korean War. The number of landlords executed has been variously estimated from 800,000 (government figure) upward to about 2 million. Many who were not killed were sent to labour camps, but the majority of those who had their land distributed remained in the villages as cultivators. Nevertheless, they had lost their political and social standing. It is noteworthy that one effect of land reform, particularly in south China, was that it undermined lineage as a social force, thus removing an alternative focus of loyalty to the regime.

POLITICAL CLASSIFICATION AND THE CAMPAIGN AGAINST COUNTER-REVOLUTIONARIES

We have seen that class labelling was an intrinsic part of land reform. While landlords and rich peasants were the obvious targets, there was scope for discretion in drawing the lines around the middle and lower-middle peasants. With the consolidation of power came the further cate-gorization of society into the proletarian class and the 'class enemies'. The proletariat included the Five Red Categories:

poor and lower-middle peasants;
workers;
revolutionary soldiers;
revolutionary cadres;
dependants of Revolutionary Martyrs.

Class enemies were the Seven Black Categories:

landlords;
rich peasants;   *Intellectual*
reactionaries;
bad elements;
rightists;
traitors;
spies.

'Intellectual' was not a designation of a class although this did not pre-vent intellectuals coming under attack, and later, notably in the Cultural Revolution they were to be described as the 'stinking ninth' category below 'capitalist roaders in authoritative positions'.

The class labels were useful in the campaigns against corruption, in the process of weeding out potential enemies of the regime and in enforcing compliance.

The campaign against counter-revolutionaries which was launched in 1950 (overlapping, as we have noted, with the attack on landlords) involved a process of public meetings, denunciations and arrests, some-times followed by executions. This mass campaign may have ferreted out a few Guomindang supporters who were trying to sabotage the new regime. It certainly terrorized millions of Chinese who, for what-ever reason, were labelled GMD sympathizers. Such figures as are available show the wide-ranging impact of the campaign. For example, in Guangdong between October 1950 and August 1951 over 140,000 were arrested and 28,332 were executed. In Tianjin in the spring of 1950 there were 492 executions, often publicly staged. Those who came under attack included the leaders of secret societies, and the members of a religious sect Yiguan Dao (The Way of Basic Unity Society.) Under pressure they recanted; in April 1951 up to 15,000 people a day were promising to give up their religion.[8]

CAMPAIGNS FOR SOCIAL CHANGE

The Party was determined to nip corruption in the bud. A campaign was launched in 1951, known as the *sanfan* (three-anti) against corruption, waste and obstructionist bureaucracy. This was followed in 1952 by the *wufan* campaign (five-anti) against bribery, tax evasion, fraud, theft of government property and of economic secrets. By public appraisal and denunciation party cadres, as well as businessmen and administrators in both the public and private sector, were held to account and frightened out of temptation. Some were punished by heavy fines, thus losing their property; some were sent to workcamps. But as a reign of terror it was modest compared with the Campaign Against Counter-revolutionaries.

The Party's high moral tone which went with its reputation for honesty also focused on social evils in the cities. Prostitution, gambling and opium addiction were effectively wiped out and the secret societies (such as the notorious Green Gang) which had fostered them and prospered were destroyed. The transformation of the cities was all the more remarkable when one considers that the Communist Party cadres had had almost no experience of administering urban areas. The fact that they were so successful so quickly in establishing effective control through neighbourhood committees and work units may well be related to the single-minded crusading zeal of cadres and converts. The Chinese tradition of collective responsibility in an extended family may have helped, together with a lack of squeamishness about spying and reporting on one's neighbour. Correction and persuasion went hand in hand. If wrongdoers were often terrorized out of their recalcitrant ways, they were sometimes offered the option of rehabilitation.

A priority was to increase literacy, in a population in which less than 20 per cent could read and write.[9] Whereas in 1949 24.4 million attended primary school, by 1953 the figure was 51.1 million. For secondary school the increase in the same period was from 1.27 million to 3.13 million.

With the Marriage Law, 30 April 1950, the new regime set out to remove women from their traditional inferior position. The new law prohibited polygamy, concubinage and child marriage. Wives were allowed to start divorce proceedings and young people were supported if they rejected an arranged marriage. Women were allowed to inherit property. In his youth Mao Zedong had campaigned against the discriminatory treatment of women[10] and now important steps were taken on the long road to raise the status of women throughout the nation.[11] Not only did the state publicly campaign for a new freedom for women, it initiated changes which directly or indirectly changed the traditional family life. The increasing number of young people who went to school and who joined new organizations such as the Young Pioneers and the New Democratic Youth League (later changed to the Communist Youth League) were less constrained by family values. Moreover, women in large numbers were drafted into the workforce. There were opportunities for women to rise within the Party and to take positions of authority in political and social organizations from street committees upwards.

The principle of religious toleration, particularly important for minority groups, was to be incorporated in the Constitution adopted in 1954 (Chapter 3). Although many foreign missionaries were to leave China within a year of Liberation, a recognized place was found for the Chinese Christians who were expected to cut their foreign links. They were registered and required to conform to the Three Selfs – freedom from foreign influence, foreign money and, specifically in the case of Roman Catholics, from Vatican control.

DEFINING THE NEW STATE

How did the Communists define their new state? They hailed a unified Chinese nation which was approximately 93 per cent Han – ethnic Chinese – and included the rest as national minorities. Over 400 groups claimed status as ethnic minorities. After investigation, over 56 were officially recognized. These included the Hui, Chinese-speaking Muslims and the Miao, scattered over several provinces, as well as the culturally and linguistically distinct provinces of Xinjiang and Tibet where the Chinese were in the minority. Five autonomous regions were created: Tibet, Xinjiang, Ningxia, Guangxi and Inner Mongolia. Other areas in Sichuan, Yunnan, Guizhou were made autonomous districts and countries. Thus local languages were recognized and respect was shown for local customs. In theory all the peoples welcomed incorporation into the People's Republic, although Tibet soon became an obvious problem.

The Communists may have expected that the Tibetans would welcome 'liberation' from what they saw as a cruel and inequitable feudal society. However, the Tibetans had a long tradition of de facto independence politically and culturally. The national religion since the twelfth century AD was the form of Buddhism know in the West as Lamaism, headed by the Dalai Lama. In 1951 an agreement signed by the fourteenth Dalai Lama provided for the continuation of the theocracy under the Chinese who set about reorganization and reforms. Territorially Tibet's northern province was made part of Qinghai while areas of eastern Tibet were incorporated into Sichuan. In the remaining Tibetan Autonomous Region the introduction of reforms was followed by rebellion, (probably with some encouragement from Taiwan and the United States) and the Dalai Lama fled to India in 1959.

How were the foreign communities in China treated by the new regime? The British government was the first non-Communist western government to recognize China on 6 January 1950 under pressure from both left-wing politicians and businessmen. As Winston Churchill put it, the reason for establishing diplomatic relations was 'not to confer a compliment but to secure a convenience'.[12] However, in spite of Mao's expressed willingness to do business with all countries and Zhou's statement 'I consider it necessary that there be established normal diplomatic relations between the People's Republic of China and all countries in the world',[13] the Chinese did not respond enthusiastically to Britain's de facto recognition. Rather than allow British diplomats to proceed with their functions they accepted them only as a negotiating mission. This went on for four years. One explanation is that Britain continued to maintain its recognition of the Republic of China on Taiwan. The Americans fared even worse. Those businessmen (and also missionaries) who were prepared to stay on experienced vituperation and harassment. The Americans blamed their own government for antagonizing the Communists but in fact the British community, who had made conciliatory gestures to meet Chinese officials and whose newspaper the *North China Daily News* meekly accepted censorship, were treated with similar disdain.

Foreigners were already on their way out a year before the Korean War led to the exodus of most of the remainder.[14]

2 'Leaning to one side', 1950–3

Within a year the People's Republic had made an alliance with the USSR and had got involved in war with the USA in Korea. Together these events influenced foreign relations and shaped the development of the country for years to come. The importance of the Korean War which confirmed China's exclusion from the United Nations and American support for the regime on Taiwan, can hardly be overstated.

The simplistic view, accepted by many at the time and for years afterwards, was that in 1949 China had 'gone over' to the Reds, had become an aggressor in Korea on behalf of world communism and had been duly punished by the United States and its allies acting in the name of the United Nations. Later Western scholarship[1] queried the inevitability of China's alliance with the USSR and suggested that American threats and actions to extend the war in Korea caused the Chinese to enter North Korea in self-defence. Recently available documentation from China and Russia has provided material for more complex interpretation.

THE PROSPECTS FOR CHINA'S FOREIGN RELATIONS IN 1949

Before we examine the Sino-Soviet Alliance of February 1950 and China's involvement in Korea in October 1950 it is instructive to examine what China's international prospects were in 1949. In April 1949 when the communist forces crossed the Yangzi at Nanjing and sent the British gunboat HMS *Amethyst* scurrying down river, both the Americans and the British were in a conciliatory mood. The British, with larger investments in China and the future of Hong Kong to consider, had more at stake and sought ways of maintaining their diplomatic status in China while seeing what could be done to salvage the position of businessmen. For a time the Truman administration was optimistic, although the National Security Council, the State Department and the Joint Chiefs of Staff did not always agree. NSC41 (28 February 1949) had argued against economic embargoes on the ground that they would be an ineffective sanction because of China's low level of consumption and, moreover, would drive China into the arms of the USSR; therefore the USA should strive 'to increase the importance to China of trade with Japan and the West.'[2] When the Nationalist capital Nanjing fell both the British ambassador and the American ambassador, Leighton Stuart, stayed on. Stuart had long experience in China and as a former Yenching University president claimed to have taught many of China's new leaders, which he believed gave him special influence since 'the relationship of teacher and student was one of the basic conceptions of Chinese ethics.' The Chinese Communist representative sent to Nanjing to deal with the western diplomats was Huang Hua, a former student at Yenching. On 6 June he impressed upon Stuart that the United States must give up any idea of supporting the Nationalists. All the CCP wanted from the US was 'the stoppage of aid and the severance of relations with the KMT (GMD) Government'.[3] This was not what the Westerners were waiting to hear. They wanted to discuss the future status of their nationals working in China, the prospects for continuing trade and to establish their diplomatic status. Then suddenly on 8 June Huang Hua sent for Philip Fugh, Stuart's personal secretary, and told him that the CCP was eager for economic recovery and American aid would be decisive.

Was there ever a realistic possibility that China with American and British economic backing might have charted an independent course from 1949 on? The decision to 'lean to one side', to depend on the friendship of the Soviet Union, was announced by Mao Zedong on 30 June 1949. 'Sitting on the fence will not do, nor is there a third road'. He reminded his listeners that China's experience over forty years indicated a preference for the side of socialism over the side of imperialism. He invoked the experience of Sun Yat-sen who in spite of countless appeals for international help only received foreign help once and that was from the Soviet Union. Mao did not dwell on the fact that on some recent occasions Soviet help had been conspicuously lacking.

Since American and British papers were duly made public in the late 1970s scholars have been intrigued by revelations of a top secret diplomatic feeler allegedly originating from Zhou Enlai himself at the end of May 1949. This 'Zhou demarche' was an oral message conveyed via an Australian journalist, Michael Keon, and an American military attaché to the American Consul General, Clubb, to the effect that the communist leadership was bitterly divided between Liu Shaoqi leading a pro-Soviet faction and Zhou Enlai who favoured links with the West. No reply was expected or indeed wanted. Nevertheless, the US State Department accepted the authenticity of the message and instructed Clubb to prepare a reply couched in general terms about 'maintaining friendly relations' for 'mutual benefit'. This reply was never delivered because no one could be found to receive it. Keon also conveyed a similar message about Zhou's allegedly Western leanings to London via Hong Kong on 10 August. At the Foreign Office the man asked to comment on this was none other than Guy Burgess – later to be unmasked as a Soviet spy. He opined that it was a trick to create a favourable impression and get concessions.[4]

By July it was clear that the US government was not about to commit itself to economic ties. The Truman administration was now convinced that it had 'lost China'. On 30 July the *China White Paper* was published. In his Letter of Transmittal Dean Acheson regretted that 'The communist leaders have foresworn their Chinese heritage and publicly announced their subservience to a foreign power'.[5] Liu Shaoqi was sent on a secret trip to Moscow and preparations were put in hand for Mao's visit in December to draw up a Sino-Soviet treaty.

A few days after Mao's 'leaning to one side' speech Lui Shaoqi was sent to Moscow, arriving on 10 July. But the Chinese did not immediately give up all hope of doing business with the West. According to Chinese sources Mao sent an emissary, Chen Mingshu, with a note to Stuart explaining his 'leaning to one side' speech and pointing out the 'difference between the political line and the stand of a state'.[6] In October the founding documents of the new regime referred to expanding trade relations in general, and later, in Moscow, Mao confided to his comrades that he still expected to trade with the capitalists including the USA.[7]

Did the mixed signals from the Chinese Communists in 1949 reflect different views among the leadership? One possible explanation is that they were orchestrated by Mao to remind the Soviets that China had alternative options. If so, this ploy was not successful. Mao got nothing from the Americans and was in danger of offending Stalin.[8]

THE SINO-SOVIET TREATY

Mao took the train to Russia on 16 December 1949. In Moscow he was bored, alternately feted and ignored by Stalin until, when the time came

Figure 2.1 Postage stamp, celebrating Sino-Soviet friendship 1950

for negotiations, he sent for Zhou Enlai. Recently released materials confirm that Mao resented the delays which are explained by Stalin's reluctance to make up his mind on the need for, and nature of, a new treaty to replace that made with Chiang Kai-shek in 1945.[9] Mao may have hoped originally that China was to be given economic rewards for 'joyously . . . following the leadership of the mighty Stalin' as Madame Sun Yat-sen (Song Qingling) enthused in January 1950.[10] If so, he was to be disappointed. Stalin pressed for concessions similar to those which had earlier been granted under duress to the imperialists. Joint stock companies were to be set up in Xinjiang and the North-east (Manchuria). Reclaiming their old interest in the Chinese Eastern Railway the Russians were reasserting the ambition of the Tsarist regime. Mao later explained on 10 March 1958 '. . . we adopted two attitudes: one was to argue when the other side made proposals we did not agree with, and the other was to accept their proposal if they absolutely insisted. This was out of consideration for the interests of socialism'.[11] Thus they agreed to Stalin's terms.[12] Three weeks after Zhou arrived, a Treaty of Friendship, Alliance and Mutual Assistance was signed on 14 February 1950. China was lent $300 million for five years at 1 per cent interest and, importantly, China was to receive Soviet technicians and Chinese personnel were sent for training in the Soviet Union. Despite the resentment the Chinese felt about their treatment, it was with a brave face that Mao told the Chinese people of the 'eternal and indestructible' friendship between the two peoples – as exhibited all over China in a joint picture of the two leaders, and commemorated in a song 'Mao Zedong! Stalin! They are shining as bright as the sun in the sky'.[13]

THE STATUS OF TAIWAN (FORMOSA)

The question of the status of Taiwan became inextricably linked with the outbreak of the Korean War. To understand this convergence we must review the origins of both.

The joint declaration of the USA, the UK and China (at Cairo 1943), which was confirmed at Potsdam in August 1945, declared that Formosa (Taiwan) which had been occupied by the Japanese since 1895 should be restored to China at the end of the war. Since the peace treaty with the Japanese had yet to be signed, this agreement was technically in abeyance. Meanwhile Chiang Kai-shek had taken refuge on the island setting up his Guomindang regime in spite of the indigenous population.

Many in the Pentagon, as well as General Douglas MacArthur of the Far East Command, were worried by the prospect of the People's Republic capturing Taiwan. However, the Pentagon also complained that it lacked the resources to defend the island. So Taiwan was to be given economic and diplomatic support while depending on its own military resources for defence. There were some in the State Department who thought of using the presence of the native Formosan population to justify permanent independence for the island. In contrast the Chinese were and always have been consistently against 'Two Chinas' or 'One China, one Taiwan'. In 1950 they lacked equipment for an amphibian invasion but their intention to take back Taiwan has never wavered.

By the spring of 1950 US policy towards the Soviet Union and China[14] was hardening. In February Senator Joseph McCarthy began his attack on 'subversives' in the State Department, which had the effect of removing all those with knowledge of or sympathy for China from any influence on US foreign policy.

THE BACKGROUND TO THE KOREAN WAR

At the end of the World War in 1945 Korea was divided at the 38th parallel into the Communist occupied North, liberated by the Russians who installed Kim Il-sung, and the South under the American sponsored Syngman Rhee. The division was not accepted by either side.

On 12 January 1950 speaking at the National Press Club, Dean Acheson, while intimating that the United States would continue to maintain its military presence in Japan, defined the US defensive perimeter in the Pacific as excluding both Taiwan and South Korea.

There was an element of wait and see in this policy; Acheson also said that aggression in Asia outside the 'perimeter' should be met by calling on 'the commitments of the entire civilized world under the Charter of the United Nations'.[15] When Kim Il-sung launched North Korean armies across the line on 25 June 1950 the Americans did just that. The Security Council in the absence of the Soviet delegates[16] who, it happened, had been withdrawn in protest at the exclusion of the People's Republic, condemned North Korea as an aggressor and a multinational United Nations force (90 per cent American) was sent just in time to prevent the whole of South Korea being overrun.

In condemning the aggression the assessment of Western governments was that the Soviet Union was culpable, if not entirely, at least in large part. Nevertheless, for decades many scholars assumed that there was a mystery about who started the Korean War. It was commonly asserted that it 'broke out' – there was some confusing evidence that a South Korean force had attacked across the parallel some hours before the massive North Korean invasion force crossed the line. Then emphasis was put on the civil war aspect and Kim Il-sung was reckoned to have taken the initiative by himself with little or no encouragement. In the 1980s 'glasnost' opened up Soviet sources and the original American contention has been partly confirmed. The Korean War started with Stalin's tacit support if not his wholehearted backing. Mao Zedong had also been told what Kim Il-sung had in mind during his visit to Moscow. The fact that neither apparently lost much sleep indicates that they thought the North Koreans could manage by themselves. They may have overestimated the strength of the DPRK (Democratic People's Republic of Korea) or misjudged the United States' reaction or both.

Recently revealed documents from both Russia and China on the origins of the war have contributed to the debate. For example, some of the visits which Kim Il-sung was alleged to have made to Moscow simply did not take place. However, there is no doubt that Kim was the driving force. He was apparently convinced that revolutionaries in the South would rise to join the North Koreans and he was optimistic about the strength of his forces in the peninsula. Nevertheless, he was realistic enough to seek to ensure a measure of approval from Stalin.

Stalin was not easily persuaded. He was preoccupied with the Sino-Soviet negotiations during the winter of 1949–50. In April Kim visited him and presented arguments that both the northern armies and southern revolutionaries were ready for a decisive attack leading to victory in three days.[17] Stalin remarked that he was more concerned with the situation in the West, and that the Koreans had better consult Mao. When

Kim did speak to Mao, the Chinese leader was preoccupied with plans for attacking Taiwan but he could hardly oppose Kim's plan. Kim presented the *fait accompli* that Stalin had accepted his argument that a southern uprising would clinch the North's victory. Meanwhile in early June China's Central Military Commission postponed the attack on Taiwan because preparations were taking longer than expected.[18] As for the timing of the North Korean invasion Mao was not informed. Chen Yi and Peng Dehuai later complained bitterly at the lack of consultation. It is noteworthy that from June to October China sent no substantial aid to the North Koreans.

At the beginning of the war (25 June 1950) there was no reason to suppose that China would be involved apart from sending messages of support. The North Korean forces seemed startlingly competent as they swept south hemming the defenders into the south-east corner of the peninsula. Of more direct importance to the Chinese was the announcement by President Truman on 27 June that the Seventh Fleet would insulate Taiwan, preventing both a communist invasion of the island and Nationalist operations against the mainland. Mao stated that this was an act of war. Beijing's plans for taking over the lost province which had just been postponed, now had to be shelved. A visit to Taiwan by the commander of the United Nations forces, Douglas MacArthur, did not go unnoticed. For the moment Mao did not make an issue of US intervention in Korea.[19]

Following a successful UN landing at Inchon on 15 September the tide was turned and the North Koreans were pushed back to the 38th parallel; MacArthur's forces prepared to push north to the Chinese border on the Yalu river. A crisis was imminent and by October Beijing was issuing warnings that China would not tolerate UN armies in North Korea. One notable message was that given by Zhou Enlai to the Indian Ambassador, K. M. Panikkar at half past midnight on 2 October, for transmission to Washington. It stated simply that if the Americans crossed the 38th parallel China would be forced to intervene in Korea.

According to a recent interpretation by Chen Jian based on Chinese sources Zhou's warning was essentially for propaganda purposes, to show China in a defensive role. Chen does not deny that MacArthur's advance threatened China but he argues that the decision to intervene was made earlier, in August, before the UN forces landed at Inchon. Mao 'treated the Korean crisis as an opportunity as well as a challenge from the beginning'.[20] Well aware of American hostility towards their regime the Communist leaders were nevertheless shocked by US intervention in Taiwan and Korea. Mao now thought that China should launch an anti-imperialist crusade. Apart from countering the American aggression it would call Stalin and the Sino-Soviet treaty to account. There were some doubts about Stalin's commitment. Also it would promote China's influence in Asia and would 'mobilize the masses'[21] by dynamically enhancing the authority of the Party and maintaining the revolutionary momentum of the Chinese people. Counter-revolutionaries had been actively spreading rumours that with American backing Chiang Kai-shek would soon be on the way back into China, and there were more than 150 acts of sabotage against the railways in the north-east province between 12 July and 11 August.[22] If action was necessary, then the mountains of Korea were as good a battlefield as any for making a stand against the Americans, reasoned Mao.

CHINA ENTERS THE WAR

However, the Chinese decision to intervene if the Americans persisted was not taken lightly. Some in the Chinese leadership, notably Chen Yun, urged that China had other priorities, a five-year plan for modernization for one, confrontation with the Nationalists for another. Those who came down on the side of intervention if necessary were Mao; Zhu De; Peng Dehuai, the head of the First Field Army and North-west military region; and Gao Gang, head of the North-east military region.

The Americans, having assessed that the Soviet Union was not going to get involved, considered that the Chinese threat might well be a bluff intended to save North Korea by offering an opening for Soviet diplomatic intervention at the UN. Nevertheless, the Chinese warning had impressed the Joint Chiefs of Staff sufficiently for them to inform MacArthur that if major Chinese units should suddenly intervene in Korea, he should continue to advance as long as 'action by your forces offers a reasonable chance of successful resistance'.[23] The underlying implication was that a Chinese army lacking armour or artillery need not be taken too seriously. MacArthur complied with this directive by submitting his plan for operations north of the 38th parallel. This was approved by the Joint Chiefs of Staff on 29 September.

On 7 October American patrols crossed the 38th parallel and on 8 October Mao having renamed the North-east Frontier Force the Chinese People's Volunteers ordered them to march speedily to Korea. Zhou Enlai and Lin Biao flew on the same day to meet Stalin at his Black Sea villa to negotiate a supply of arms. Stalin pointed out that

China should help the North Koreans. Otherwise it would be in danger; if it failed to fight in Korea it would have to fight the Americans in north-east China. The Soviet Union could not enter the war without creating a third world war. Some Soviet weapons could be supplied, including some aircraft provided they did not antagonize world opinion by operating 'behind the enemy's rear'. The Chinese delegates, dismayed, went on to Moscow where, within hours, they were informed by Molotov that Stalin had changed his mind; he did not think that China should send in troops, and would not supply military equipment.[24]

When Mao got this news he reportedly spent a sleepless seventy hours thinking about it. On the 13th he cabled Zhou Enlai reiterating the reasons for going to war. The Chinese crossed the Yalu river into North Korea on 19 October. At first, without air cover, they suffered appalling losses from US air strikes. Later Stalin did send some arms and munitions, and allowed China additional financial credit to pay for them.[25]

In the event the Chinese forces achieved, though at great loss of life, an astounding success. On 24 November MacArthur announced the beginning of an offensive to end the war but within days his broken forces were fleeing south. By January 1951 they had recrossed the 38th parallel into South Korea. When the UN forces regrouped and counterattacked they were unable to move far. By July a stalemate had been reached approximately along the line of the 38th parallel which was recognized in the negotiations for a ceasefire (July 1951) but it was a further two years before an armistice was signed on 27 July 1953. Even to this day, pending a peace settlement, the countries are technically still at war.

China's entry into the Korean War resulted in the United States severing all ties with China. The United States Senate resolved (on 23 January 1951) that the United Nations should declare Communist China an aggressor in Korea, which it did on 1 February, and that the Beijing regime should not be admitted to the United Nations as the representative of China. Before the end of 1950 American restrictions on trade with China, first introduced in 1949, were extended to a complete embargo. Not only did the Truman administration stop all imports and exports to and from China, it also blocked Chinese owned assets in the US and sought to prevent the transhipment of US exports to China. Thus began the policy, maintained until 1971, of isolating Communist China diplomatically and economically. All those nations susceptible to US influence were pressed to conform.

The consequences of the Korean War can hardly be overestimated. The 'limited war' of salvation caused immense destruction throughout the peninsula and particularly in the north where at least 12 per cent of the population were killed. Millions more were displaced. The extent of the destruction curdled the stomach of General MacArthur himself. He testified 'After I looked at that wreckage and those thousands of women and children and everything, I vomited'.[26]

The Chinese casualties were at least 366,000[27] including Mao's eldest son; China's resources were diverted from reconstruction at home. Plans for the conquest of Taiwan were set back indefinitely while Chiang Kai-shek at the cost of a few commando raids on the mainland became the firm ally of the United States. US aid was stepped up with the decision to 'unleash' Chiang Kai-shek in February 1953 and on 2 December 1954 the United States signed a mutual defence treaty with the regime on Taiwan. Japan also did well out of the war, which was directed from bases in Japan and gave a tremendous stimulus to the Japanese economy. The long-delayed peace treaty between the US and Japan was signed in 1951.

On the other hand the Chinese gained significantly in prestige. Their 'volunteers' had confronted the highly developed military power of the United States and had forced it to a stalemate. Some Americans had learnt the lesson that Red China was not to be interfered with; there was less talk of backing a Nationalist liberation of the mainland. As to relations with the USSR, the war had superficially at least confirmed China as a member of the Soviet block but at a price. Moreover, the Chinese did not forget the niggardliness of the Soviets who sent China the bill for supplies while withholding their best equipment. In 1997, Chinese academics rewriting the history of the war showed that after Stalin's death Mao repeatedly complained that the Korean War had been a big mistake – '100 per cent wrong'.[28]

3 The politics of the People's Republic, 1953–7

The Chinese followed Soviet examples both economically in their five-year plan and politically in their constitution. In the course of institutionalizing their rule the Communist leaders continued to defer to Mao. However, in the aftermath of Khrushchev's denunciation of Stalin (February 1956) the Party leadership at the Eighth Party Congress in September 1956 relegated Mao to a less dominant position. He fought back, pressed successfully for more rapid co-operativization in agriculture and appeared to be encouraging the intellectuals in his call for freedom of expression. Those who took up Mao's invitation to 'let a hundred flowers bloom' were soon castigated as poisonous weeds. Was this a trap to get dissidents to reveal themselves?

INSTITUTIONALIZING CONTROL: THE CONSTITUTION

The Communists had been running the People's Republic for five years, when in September 1954 the temporary arrangements for governing China made in 1949 were replaced by a formal constitution: the facade of state structures within which the Communist Party would go on exercising power. Article 1 described China as a People's Democracy. China had not yet made the transition to socialism (total state control of the economy) and the ultimate goal of communism, distribution according to needs, was still distant.

The general line for the transition to socialism, announced in October 1953, provided for the gradual change of the united front policy. During the stage of 'state capitalism' the capitalists would come increasingly under state control but would retain some of their profits. For the bourgeoisie the writing was on the wall, but as Liu Shaoqi said in September 1954, they could be dealt with 'by peaceful means'.

A pyramid of People's Congresses extended upwards from the 'voting masses' (the franchise was given to all men and women over 18 except

---

State Council
Premier, Deputy Premiers and Ministers
The executive body, at head of
government apparatus. Oversees work
of departments. Almost all are also
members of the Party Central Committee

**Standing Committee of
National People's Congress**
140 members
Many of its members are key party officers.
• supervises election to NPC
• interprets laws
• oversees work of State Council, supreme
 court and supreme procuratorate
• issues decrees in certain areas between
 NPC meetings.
Acts largely as a rubber stamp for the
Party executive.

- - - - - - - - - - - - - - - - - - -

National People's Congress
Up to 3,000 members elected every
five years or less.
Meets annually for up to 15 days.

Provincial People's Congresses

County People's Congresses

Electorate
All over 18 years old

Note: Power is exercised from the top through
 the selection of candidates and the
 control of elections.

Figure 3.1 The state (simplified)

convicted criminals and enemies of the state). At the local level representatives were elected to the provincial level from which representatives were elected to the National People's Congress. There they were joined by representatives from the national minorities and from the armed forces. The delegates of the NPC were to meet for two weeks every year. When they were not in session, power was exercised by the permanent Standing Committee, which, in theory, supervised the executive government, appointed judges to the Supreme People's Court and prepared and conducted elections. Above the Standing Committee was the State Council, consisting of the Premier, Deputy Premiers, ministers and chairmen of commissions, and above the State Council was the head of state, the President/Chairman of the People's Republic of China. (The Chinese term *zhuxi* is translated as either Chairman or President.) In September 1954 Mao Zedong was elected to this newly created post.

In contrast to the theoretical federalism of the Soviet Union, the People's Republic of China was established as a unitary state. The national autonomous regions were inalienable parts of the Republic and could not legally secede. The NPC Standing Committee and the State Council had powers to exercise a veto over all local provinces, autonomous regions and municipalities.

The constitution followed the 1936 Soviet model in setting up a theoretically independent judicial system of courts and people's prosecutors. There was a list of citizens' rights and duties similar to that in the Soviet constitution; one difference, that the Chinese did not postulate a secret ballot, was explained by the fact that conditions in China were different.[1]

In effect this structure was designed for control from the top. This would not necessarily imply blind obedience. Indeed, the Maoist adage 'From the people to the people' envisaged a two-way traffic in ideas. In practice, although there was scope for local participation in politics, this did not mean that the masses would regularly formulate demands and forward them to the government. Rather, the people were instructed and marshalled behind Party policies. There was nothing strange in this concept. It simply institutionalized the principle of 'democratic centralism' also practised in other communist countries.

This constitution, in contrast to the legal frameworks of Western countries, was not intended to give independence to private citizens by fixing limits to state power. Indeed its provisions were always liable to be changed or even ignored in the interests of the highest authority. The first constitution lasted until 1975, the second until 1978, the third until 1982. Successive constitutions reflected shifts in the political balance.

THE PARTY

As in the Soviet Union, the Party organization was in parallel with the machinery of government. The members of the Party were represented in the Party Congress which has met at irregular intervals since the founding Party Congress in 1921.[2] The central Party structure, which became institutionalised in the new state, has remained virtually

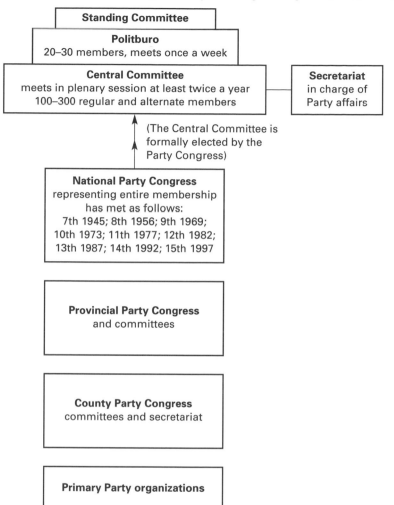

Figure 3.2 The Party (simplified)

unchanged until the present. The Congress formally elects a Central Committee with 100 to 300 members and alternate non-voting members, including leading officials, experts, and representatives, i.e. model peasants or workers. The Central Committee formally elects a Politburo with between 20 and 30 members which meets regularly. This is the powerhouse which dominates and controls the Party and makes key governmental decisions. At the 'plenary sessions' (or 'plenums') of the

Central Committee important policy decisions have usually been made at the behest of the Politburo. Within the Politburo there is a smaller group, the Standing Committee (which makes general and overriding decisions). In early 1956, for example, this consisted of Mao Zedong, Liu Shaoqi, Zhu De, Zhou Enlai and Chen Yun.

The Party centre in Beijing extended its control through a hierarchy of territorially based organizations and of party 'fractions' in government, education, factories, agriculture, the armed forces, and all walks of life. Party fractions, the dominant element in the social units to which every one was attached, such as the work unit and the street committee, provided a very effective means of surveillance, preventing crime, enforcing social sanctions, overseeing welfare needs, and organizing campaigns for ideological correctness. Between 1949 and 1955 Party membership increased from 4.5 million to 10 million. It was used as a reward for loyalty and merit.

Mass organizations were used by the Party as an important instrument of control and popular mobilization behind Party goals. Originally set up in 1949 these bodies had come to encompass large sections of the population. By 1953 the trade unions, an important instrument of propaganda, numbered 12 million, the New Democratic Youth League had 9 million and the Women's Federation formally numbered 76 million. One purpose of mass mobilization, as Mao noted in 1955,[3] was to create a sense of national unity.

The experiences of China's leaders throughout the revolutionary period had been closely linked to the military. In 1949 the Communist forces (land, sea and air) were brought together into the People's Liberation Army. The PLA was under the control of the Party's Military Affairs Commission, which was always chaired by Mao Zedong although run routinely by a Vice-Chairman. Since the PLA leaders ranked equally with the State Council (see above) the government could not dominate the military.[4] The party was not only able to use the military for protection, it could also use the military for promoting party objectives, as well as, or instead of, using the government bureaucracy. In Mao Zedong's China many of the Party's top leaders were either military officers or had strong connections with the military.

INSTITUTIONALIZING WEAKNESSES: A FLAWED SYSTEM AT TOP AND BOTTOM

Kenneth Lieberthal has noted that China's political system is inherently flawed at the top and bottom. At the top, despite all the regulations written into the constitution, two to three dozen officials are virtually unrestrained in an unregulated relationship. Their power struggles create instability which is liable to upset the entire system of government.[5]

At the bottom the population has been deprived of effective political participation. The people were there to be mobilized to serve causes, whether 'struggling' against class enemies, or promoting agricultural reform. They were not given the opportunity to practise self-government free from the overbearing hand of the Party. This means that popular protest, when it does occur, erupts as unruly demonstrations and street violence. If this was inevitable in the early transition years of the People's Republic, it has had a deleterious effect on further political development, leaving China with an immature, underdeveloped political system.

THE SOVIET STYLE FIVE-YEAR PLAN

By the Sino-Soviet Treaty of February 1950 the two countries had undertaken 'to develop and consolidate economic and cultural ties . . .' and 'to render the other all possible economic assistance and to carry out necessary economic co-operation'.[6] At first China's limited planning capabilities, ongoing negotiations with the Soviet Union, and the demands of the Korean War forestalled a full-scale plan for industrialization. It was discussed during a visit to Moscow in autumn 1952 by Zhou Enlai and Chen Yun, with Stalin himself setting the industrial growth rate figure for China.[7] Then, in September 1953 after the Korean armistice, the Chinese produced the blueprint for a Soviet-style five-year plan with emphasis on the development of heavy industry. The final version was not published until April 1955.

There was broad agreement on accepting the Soviet model. This entailed centralized planning and direction, including the setting of production targets. Although it was an urban-oriented strategy for development, there is little to suggest that Mao and his comrades deemed it incompatible with their experience in the countryside. Rather, they recognized that with the capture of the cities the time had come to move on to a higher stage of revolutionary development. As consideration was given to how best to adapt the new strategies to the Chinese situation, there was some limited debate which led to general consensus. As Mao said later, 'In the early stages of nationwide liberation we lacked the experience to administer the economy of the entire country. Therefore during the First Five-Year Plan we could only imitate the methods of the Soviet Union'.[8] This seems to overlook the fact that the

Chinese Communist Party had long been following many of the basic organizational principles and methods of the Soviets. In any case there was no single Soviet model. The most recent was the Soviet Fourth Five-Year Plan of 1946–50. This model had been formulated in the harsh post-war period. Its techniques, described as 'High Stalinism', were accepted and applied by the Chinese; for example, they took the Seven Precepts of Management with their emphasis on mass campaigns to boost production. What the Chinese did not appreciate was that this method had been secretly dropped by the Soviets in 1947 because it was too disruptive of working patterns. If, as has been suggested in a recent study,[9] the technique of industrial management in China was distorted by the acceptance of an extreme Stalinist model, it is hard to picture the CCP being impelled to extreme measures against its will. However, while the top leadership embarked on the Russian course with their eyes open, it is likely that lesser officials and party functionaries were carried unquestioningly along by the propaganda image of the respected 'elder brother'.

The years 1953–7 saw some remarkable progress in heavy industry and mining. By 1957 the North-east provinces (Manchuria) had more than regained their former level of production. Similarly the industry of Shanghai and Wuhan had expanded. A noteworthy achievement, which for the first time linked north and south without a ferry, was the building of road and rail bridges across the Yangzi at Wuhan. Geological exploration revealed reserves of oil, uranium and other valuable minerals in Xinjiang and elsewhere.

The success of the Five-Year Plan depended on Soviet expertise. Approximately 10,000 Soviet and East European experts were working in China, while thousands of Chinese technicians were sent for training in the USSR. However, the Chinese were responsible for financing the programme; Soviet loans had to be repaid and by 1955 China was paying back more than it was receiving.

Inflation, held in check by the People's Bank (established in December 1948), was subject to further controls during the potentially inflationary period of the Korean War. A landmark was reached in 1955 when the old currency was exchanged at 10,000 to one for a new yuan. A remarkable level of stability had been achieved which was to last for two decades.

Individual businesses which had remained in private hands under state supervision were eventually transferred to joint private/state ownership until by 1956 all large enterprises were either state controlled or under joint ownership. In many cases the former owners remained as managers while a fixed return on capital of 5 per cent was permitted.

Although this was later reduced to 3.3 per cent, the principle of private property investment remained in place until the Cultural Revolution. Light industry and the production of consumer goods had low priority at this time. Agriculture had to bear the main burden of the costs of heavy industry: the price of grain sold to the state was fixed to produce a large profit for the state which together with taxation provided the necessary surplus. Therefore the process of agricultural reform was crucial.

AGRICULTURE

We have seen (Chapter 1) that the revolution in the countryside had destroyed the gentry as a class and in redistributing the land had implemented a peasant's dream of tilling his own land.

The leadership, facing the overriding problem of increasing agricultural production both to feed a growing population and provide the resources to support industrialization, saw the need to achieve efficiency and economy of scale through socialist organization.

The initial decision to set up agricultural co-operatives had been made in December 1951, while the peasants were still flush with the joy of gaining the land from the exploiters. It was believed that a fragmented peasant economy could not deliver the necessary increase in production. However, those Communist leaders who knew their economic history were aware of the dire effects of Stalin's precipitous measures of collectivization. It was therefore intended that there should be a gradual change beginning with the introduction of mutual aid teams. In these, peasants pooled their animals, tools and labour, at first at harvest times and, later, on a year round basis. This was already the accepted practice in many parts of China and indeed in other countries. As an effective and generally acceptable way of pooling resources it was an appropriate development. It was realized that really large scale production would need many tractors at a time when no tractors were being made in China and few people knew what a tractor looked like. By early 1955 about 65 per cent of peasant households belonged to mutual aid teams and the next stage in the transition was already under way.

The second stage was the setting-up of agricultural producers co-operatives (APCs) in which the land was worked as a single unit. The villagers were remunerated in proportion to what they had contributed, whether it was land, tools or labour or a combination of all three. Points were awarded, which were assessed for credit in grain or money when the harvest was in and the state had taken its share as well as bought a quota at fixed prices.

On 16 December 1953 the Central Committee of the CCP had passed a new resolution on agriculture producers co-operatives and by June 1955 they had grown to encompass 16.9 million peasant households out of a total 110 million. At this point Mao intervened. He was concerned that the transition had not been going as well as expected. Some of the better-off peasants were dragging their feet; the inexperience and incompetence of many rural party cadres have also been cited as a reason for failure. In 1953 and 1954 the grain production was estimated to have risen by less than 2 per cent; other crops such as cotton did even less well. This was incompatible with the need of China's growing population for food and clothes and with the requirements of light industry for raw materials from the countryside.

What was wrong? Some, the gradualists, felt that China was not ready for the APCs; it lacked the prerequisites for large-scale farming, such as tractors and chemical fertilizers. Among these doubters were such leading figures as Liu Shaoqi and Zhou Enlai. An able official Deng Zihui (1896–1972), head of the Central Committee's Rural Work Department, was actually working to reduce the number of APCs in 1955. Then on 31 July 1955 Mao delivered a speech castigating those who wanted to proceed slowly like tottering women with bound feet. The debate was over (as Chen Yi one of the moderates remarked resignedly).

The Central Committee decreed that a higher stage, full co-operatives, in effect collectives in which members would be remunerated only for their labour, should be established by April 1958. Enthusiastic cadres in the countryside were anxious to prove their worth; by the end of 1957 the initial process of co-operativization was virtually complete. The stage was set for the co-operatives to become collectives.

PROBLEMS OF MODERNIZATION

By the mid-1950s there were two fundamental problems: the strategy of economic development and the role of the intellectuals, which led to disagreement within the top leadership. These issues combined to mark a watershed in the history of the People's Republic.

As we have seen, the First Five-Year Plan, with its mixed record of achievement, had to be evaluated and considered in context with the controversial programme for rural co-operativization. Heavy industrial production showed a higher growth rate than light industry (as planned) but agriculture was relatively disappointing. Although there had been overall growth from a low base and the majority of the population had clearly benefited, the leadership was divided on the way ahead.

The early years of the People's Republic had seen the suppression of dissent and the enforcement of conformity. Those who had been tamed in this way, China's intellectuals, were relatively few in number but in the context of a drive for modernization could not be ignored. We have seen (Chapter 1) that in the three antis and the five antis (campaigns) anti-social behaviour and subversive elements had been identified and dealt with more often than not by 'remoulding'. There was a rationale for strictly enforcing conformity, during and immediately after the civil war and during the Korean War but this became less acceptable as the country settled into a period of peace with promises of wellbeing. It was an appropriate time to reconsider policy towards the intellectuals.

In 1955 a measure of the pressure to conform ideologically is seen in the attack on the writer and critic Hu Feng (1903–85), formerly a close associate of Lu Xun. A member of the National People's Congress, Hu Feng wrote to the Central Committee complaining of what he called the 'five daggers' aimed at the heart of Chinese literature. He objected to the requirement that the sole source of inspiration should be the lives of workers and peasants; that the Party was dictating both the subjects and the forms of literature; and that writers had to accept Communist ideology and be subject to thought reform.

The attack on Hu Feng was spearheaded by an anonymous article in the *People's Daily* written by Mao himself. After this China's most distinguished writers rushed to condemn the man who had been brave enough to speak up and no doubt learnt their lesson when he was forthwith imprisoned.[10]

This example was likely to inhibit intellectuals from a wholehearted engagement in the new ideas necessary for modernization. Barely had Hu been put away than the country's top scientists were convened in Beijing in June 1955 to discuss long-term research. Zhou Enlai addressed the meeting for an hour and a half delineating the role of science in new China in a way which would not deter the scientists. The following January (14th) Zhou made a keynote speech reiterating that intellectuals would be well treated and trusted; henceforth, whatever their origins the great majority would be considered as part of the working class. In return they must give due attention to ideological reform. Meanwhile the Party would allow time as Zhou explained – 'if they are prepared to devote their knowledge and energies to serving the people, we must be able to wait for the gradual awakening of their consciousness and help them patiently while at the same time criticizing their wrong ideology'.[11] Zhou suggested that more intellectuals should be allowed into the Party; as a result the number of intellectuals rose by 50 per cent in the next year.[12] When Mao presented his new agricultural programme to the Politburo in December 1955, he spoke of the need for the co-operation of intellectuals in the life of the country. He saw the need for an active intellectual force which could not only remove dependence on Soviet experts but which could also help to by-pass bureaucratic channels. Mao was beginning to show his disenchantment with the Soviet model. We now see that this was the beginning of a new Maoist road – an indicator of new Maoist policies.

At this point a bombshell was thrown into the ideological arena in February 1956, when the new Soviet leader Nikita Khrushchev denounced Stalin at the Twentieth Congress of the Communist Party of the Soviet Union. The shock waves reverberated across the whole political spectrum. Having publicly at least acknowledged Stalin as the leader of the Communist world with China in the role of younger brother, Mao resented the lack of prior consultation. Moreover, Khrushchev's reassessment of Stalin was quite unacceptable. The Chinese Party issued its own statement on 5 April: 'on the historical experience of the dictatorship of the proletariat'. This largely devilified Stalin, 'an outstanding Marxist–Leninist fighter' and pointed out that the problem of the 'personality cult' he was supposed to have fostered was not relevant to China where the order of the day was collective leadership and democratic centralism featuring the 'mass line'.

In a speech 'On the ten major relationships' on 25 April 1956 (not officially published until 1977) Mao simplistically said that Stalin's achievement outweighed his mistakes by 7 to 3. He went on to analyse the particular problems facing China, some of which had been exacerbated by slavishly following the Soviet Union. He suggested that giving more attention to developing light industry and agriculture would not only meet the needs of the people but would also provide funds for investment in heavy industry. This led to some adjustment of the investment ratio between heavy and light industry and to rethinking what investment would eventually be required for agriculture in the Second Five-Year Plan. He also questioned the Soviet model of maintaining centralized control by economic ministries and giving power to one manager in a factory. He considered that these factors enhanced the role of the experts over that of the Party.

On 2 May Mao tossed a little bomb of his own into the political debate, with the slogan 'Let a hundred flowers bloom. Let a hundred schools of thought contend.' In fact the full explosion came later. For the time being most writers, artists and scientists were wary of reacting to this challenge.

THE EIGHTH PARTY CONGRESS

The controversies came to a head in September 1956 when the Party held its Eighth Congress, the first congress since it had come to power and eleven years after the Seventh Congress in 1945. Membership of the Party had grown approximately tenfold (from 1.2 million to 10.7 million). While the criteria for membership remained commitment to the avowed aims of the Party, the actual motivation was questionable. The advantages of party membership in post-liberation society might well have appealed to those for whom personal advancement was paramount.

For the first five years after liberation China's political leaders had been generally united. The exceptions were Gao Gang and Rao Shushi, who were both purged in 1954, apparently for attempting to supplant Zhou Enlai and Lui Shaoqi. Gao was accused of separatist ambitions in the North-east, of pro-Soviet inclinations and his extreme adherence to the Soviet development model which happened to favour his heavily industrialized fief in the North-east. The departure of Gao strengthened the hand of those opposed to Soviet-style systems in China. When in March 1955 the 'campaign to wipe out hidden counter-revolutionaries' was launched it was related to the need to remove Gao and Rao's supporters as well as to reassert the control of the Party over the bureaucrats who had risen to political and economic power with the Five-Year Plan.[13]

At the Eighth Party Congress, only a few months after Khrushchev's attack on Stalin, the question of personal versus collective leadership was about to surface in China. At the Congress Mao was relegated to a less dominant position. By the new party constitution Mao was no longer *ex officio* Chairman of the Central Committee, the Politburo or the Secretariat. Liu Shaoqi as First Vice-Chairman exercised many of the executive functions of the Central Committee, and Deng Xiaoping, the new General Secretary of the Party, was also Chairman of the Secretariat. Mao's thought was no longer described as the doctrine of the Chinese Communist movement.

The new six member Standing Committee of the Politburo (formerly a five member secretariat) collectively made decisions which had previously been Mao's. However, as head of state as well as chairman of the

Party, Mao still had the main voice and was not about to abdicate his perceived responsibilities.

At issue also at the Congress was the speed of the move towards 'higher level' agricultural producers co-operatives, (in effect collectives) which had begun in October 1955. Zhou Enlai, Vice-Chairman of the Party and Premier of the State Council, supported by his planning officials, who criticized impetuosity and adventurism and the setting of unrealistic targets, was arguing in the summer of 1956 that key projects must be co-ordinated so that they allowed for actual conditions in different regions and in different sectors of the economy. Zhou also argued that financial planning was essential and should not be blindly dismissed as a cover for 'financial limitations'. He stressed the importance of developing stockpiling techniques to provide reserves. To persuade Mao and Liu Shaoqi, who both wished to maintain the speed of development, Zhou presented reports from provincial party secretaries criticizing the effects of the 1956 leap forward, sometimes called the 'little great leap'. First secretary Jiang Weiqing of Jiangsu said the cadres had become too bossy. They boasted 'we have the cooperative members by their pigtails, and from now on we'll be able to do things well'. As a result targets had been too high and too many duties were assigned to the co-operatives.[14]

Mao seems to have been genuinely self-effacing at the time of the Congress, perhaps in reaction to the problems of the 'little great leap' in agriculture, perhaps on reflecting on the moral of Stalin's 'personality cult'; he seems to have considered the advantages of devolving some of his power and influence. However, this phase in his thinking did not persist for very long.

THE 'HUNDRED FLOWERS' BLOOM

When Mao addressed the Central Committee in November he spoke of the need to win the support of the masses (and the cadres) who were liable to be overwhelmed by the experts. Perhaps he was implying that the 1956 rebellions in Poland and Hungary came from ignoring the people, in particular the intellectuals?[15] On the theme of what he called 'great democracy' he said:

If you alienate yourself from the masses and fail to solve their problems, the peasants will wield their carrying poles, the workers will demonstrate in the streets and the students will create disturbances. Whenever such things happen, they must in the first place be taken as good things, and that is how I look at the matter.

He complained that a party of students had been prevented from bringing their grievances to Beijing. Not only should the students have been allowed to visit the departments concerned but the 'workers should be allowed to go on strike and the masses to hold demonstrations; processions and demonstrations are provided for in our constitution. In the future when the constitution is revised. I suggest that the freedom to strike be added'.[16]

In a speech to businessmen and factory owners at the end of the year Mao congratulated them on their political reform. In January he informed the editor of the magazine *Poetry* that it could publish his poems which mostly followed the classical style. Was this intended to charm the intellectuals? In a talk to party secretaries at the beginning of 1957 Mao lashed out at party cadres 'who now scramble for fame and fortune and are interested only in personal gain'.[17]

It was on 27 February 1957 that Mao delivered his ideas on freedom of speech (outside the Party) in a long speech to 1800 people. 'On the correct handling of contradictions among the people' did not have the approval of Mao's colleagues. One student commented, 'eighty per cent of the high ranking cadres disapproved and some of them even got up and walked out of the meeting' (It lasted four hours!)[18] Some tape recordings of the speech circulated around China and extracts were published in the *New York Times* but it was not until 19 June that an official version was published in the *People's Daily* , which was significantly more left-wing in tone than the original February version, as a new anti-rightist campaign had begun. Mao distinguished between antagonistic contradictions (between the people and the 'enemy') and non-antagonistic contradictions (among the people) which could be resolved.

An upshot was a lively period of 'blooming and contending'. Long after Mao's original call for free speech he was at last being taken seriously. In fact there was a furore of criticism which was greater than he had bargained for. At first Mao defended the freedom of discussion: even commenting that not many Shanghai workers had taken part. But by the end of June it was over. Those who had spoken out found themselves castigated as 'poisonous weeds'. As the victims of the new anti-rightist campaign they suffered variously by demotion and exile.

Was this a fiasco? Did the movement get out of hand? Was it a cunning ploy to get dissidents to reveal themselves? This was the explanation favoured by the Party. It implies that the Communist Party knew what it was doing: that it was in control all along.

Given the soul-searching within the leadership over the past year and having regard to Mao's track record as the pacemaker it seems sounder to examine his motives. It has been suggested that these can best be understood by his frequent reference to the need for immunization against disease. He believed that the Hungarian uprising which had threatened the rule of the government party had been a reaction against years of repressing free speech. Allowing a campaign of criticism in China which could be contained would lead to better relations with 'the masses' who would thus be effectively inoculated against further serious outbreaks.[19]

It must also be seen in the context of Mao's disdain for the Party and bureaucrats: his desire not only to reassert himself but to hold high the principles of revolution in which he above all others still believed. It was a slap in the face for the party leadership and, although they did not know it, a foretaste of what was to come in the Cultural Revolution.

4 China's independent road, 1954–64

In the ten years from 1954 to 1964 the People's Republic, while remaining excluded from the United Nations, and with its trade restricted by the American enforced embargoes, experienced increasing difficulties in its relations with the Soviet Union and the Communist bloc. Indeed by 1960 the extent of China's isolation was highlighted by the fact that its only ideological ally was tiny Albania. Contemporaneously with these developments, China began to appear in a new role as a leader of the non-aligned countries in the Third World. In the mid-1950s the keynote was 'peaceful coexistence'. By the 1960s, in competition with both Soviet and American influence, the Chinese attempted to create a third force in which militant anti-imperialism sometimes went hand in hand with trade and 'mutual benefit'.

CHINA'S DIPLOMATIC ROLE, 1953–5

Having saved the face, and indeed the Cold War position of the Soviet Union, and having fought the United States to a draw in Korea, China might well have been riding high. In 1954 China was to play a prominent part at the Geneva Conference which began by dealing with Korea and went on to consider the problem of Indochina consequent on the collapse of French power. The Chinese delegation led by Zhou Enlai ranked with the other four great powers and had a considerable impact on the settlement. Why did China, having given military aid to the Vietminh, persuade them to back down at Geneva?

The Indochinese leader Ho Chi Minh had had little contact with Mao Zedong while they were both involved in liberating their own countries. Ho had founded the Vietminh (the League for the Independence of Vietnam) in 1941 but by 1949 he was still far from throwing out the French colonialists. In January 1950 he visited Beijing and was welcomed by Liu Shaoqi who stated '. . . it is our international obligation to support the anti-French struggle of the Vietnamese people' even though Liu expected that this would cause the French to postpone recognition of the People's Republic of China.[1] Ho went on with China's blessing to Moscow, where the Sino-Soviet Treaty was being negotiated, eventually travelling back with Mao and Zhou in February.

While Stalin was prepared to recognize Ho's government he was loathe to offer direct financial aid. There is some evidence that Stalin offered Mao the responsibility for supporting the Vietminh.[2] A rationale for this was that it fitted both the Chinese model of revolution in the countryside, and the concept that the Chinese revolution offered an example to be followed by the oppressed peoples of Asia and the world. In any case the PRC and the Vietminh had a common interest in the bordering regions of south China and north Indo-China where some Chinese nationalist forces had taken refuge. A Chinese adviser, General Chen Geng, went to Vietnam in late July 1950 and directed the Vietminh campaign which drove the French out of their bases near the northern frontier. Ho Chi Minh called this 'a triumph of proletarian internationalism'[3] and asked Chen to stay in Vietnam for the next campaign, but Chen was recalled in November and by the following year he was in Korea as deputy commander of the Chinese People's Volunteers. Although China was concentrating its efforts in Korea, the Vietminh did benefit from Chinese advice. In the famous campaign which broke the French forces at Dien Bien Phu were four Vietminh battalions trained and armed with anti-aircraft guns by the Chinese. The Chinese also taught the Vietnamese techniques of engineering and sniping which had been developed in Korea.[4] According to one Chinese source China provided the Vietminh with 116,000 guns and 4,360 cannon between 1950 and 1954.[5] Throughout this period China kept a low profile; it maintained a diplomatic distance, not sending an official envoy to the DRV until September 1954 after the Geneva Agreements.

- The Geneva Conference had been convened at the suggestion of the USSR to deal with both Korea and Indochina. On 8 May 1954 it was due to turn its attention to Indochina. On 7 May came the colossal defeat of the French army at Dien Bien Phu.

The Americans, confronted with the French defeat, were in an impasse and the Chinese, who had their own motives, helped them to get out of it. Ho Chi Minh, stating that peace could be obtained only by total victory, was not keen on multilateral negotiations involving all the great powers, and in November he proposed bilateral negotiations with the French.[6] But at Geneva China played the leading part in getting the Vietnamese to the international conference and pressuring them to accept less than they hoped for and were entitled to expect on the basis of the military position. Zhou Enlai first sounded out Pierre Mendès-France, the newly elected French premier, who had committed himself to ending the war and offered him a face-saving agreement involving the partition of Vietnam. Zhou then persuaded the Vietminh to accept this and also the division of the country at the 17th rather than the 16th parallel saying 'after the French withdrawal, the whole of Vietnam will be yours'.[7] The armistice was signed on 21 July 1954.

With the (supposedly temporary) division of the country the DRV was promised that elections would be held in two years which would lead, they imagined, to the unification of the country. In pressing for a negotiated settlement Zhou Enlai was anxious not to give the Americans an excuse to intervene militarily. He had therefore worked for a consensus between all the other participants which would isolate the US. In the event the Americans held back from signing the Geneva accords while undertaking not to disturb the arrangements. Within two years they had done just that, helping Ngo Dinh Diem (appointed Premier of South Vietnam on 16 June 1954 by Bao Dai) to consolidate an American backed regime. Because it was believed the North would win a majority of votes, the national election was never held and the scene was set for the American war in Vietnam in the 1960s.[8]

Zhou Enlai seems to have felt badly about what happened. He accepted that he had been 'personally responsible for urging the Vietnamese to go along with the agreement'.[9] In 1971 when an American journalist asked him if he would be willing to mediate between the United States and North Vietnam he declined saying 'We were very badly taken in during the first Geneva Conference'.[10] As for the Vietnamese, at the time of the Chinese invasions in 1979 they stated that in 1954 'the Chinese leaders betrayed the revolutionary struggles of the peoples of Vietnam, Laos and Kampuchea'.

AMERICAN SUPPORT FOR TAIWAN: THE QUESTION OF UNLEASHING CHIANG KAI-SHEK

In July 1954 both China and the USA were taking steps to consolidate their positions. During a break in the Geneva Conference, 21 June to 9 July, Zhou Enlai had called to see Pandit Nehru and together they endorsed the Five Principles of Peaceful Coexistence (first discussed in December 1953)

1   Mutual respect for each other's territorial integrity and sovereignty;
2   Non-aggression;
3   Non-interference in each other's internal affairs;
4   Equality and mutual benefit;
5   Peaceful co-existence.

These were to become the touchstone of China's relations with the emerging ex-colonial countries of the Third World. By April 1955, at the conference of Afro-Asian heads of state at Bandung, Zhou Enlai sought to uphold the image of China as a peacemaker and to dispel any anxiety that China would play an aggressive role. On the question of Taiwan, he offered to negotiate with the United States.

For their part the Americans were fearful of subversion aimed at undermining the anti-communist regimes, particularly in South-east Asia. This was a main motive behind the setting up of the South-east Asia Treaty Organization in September 1954. The United States, Britain, France, Australia and New Zealand joined with the Philippines, Thailand and Pakistan to form a joint defence system against Communist aggression either overt or subversive.

The United States also had to decide how far it was prepared to support the ambitions of Chiang Kai-shek who had dedicated his GMD regime to reclaiming the mainland of China. The question of 'unleashing' Chiang Kai-shek arose when, on 3 February 1953, the incoming American President Eisenhower in his State of the Union message announced that the United States Seventh Fleet would 'no longer be employed to shield Communist China' from possible Nationalist attacks. He was careful to add 'this order implies no aggressive intent on our part'. Nevertheless the Nationalists welcomed the statement. Their ambassador in Washington, Wellington Koo called on the Assistant Secretary of State and let it be known that the Nationalists would step up their raids on the mainland. The GMD was hoping to provoke a communist response which would lead to increased American backing.

Taiwan was not covered by SEATO and the United States made a separate defensive alliance, the Mutual Security pact on 2 December 1954. This in effect brought Chiang Kai-shek under control again. Nevertheless it provoked a protest in the *People's Daily* editorial entitled 'China will liberate Taiwan'. As so often with such polemics the text did not mention any specific plans for invading Taiwan but was concerned with condemning the alleged aggressive nature of the pact, focusing on Article 6 which provides that the scope of armed action 'will be applicable to such other territories as may be determined by mutual agreement'.[11] American and British protestations that the pact was essentially defensive and peaceful were scornfully dismissed.

The tiny islands of Jinmen and Mazu, still held by the Nationalists only a few miles from the mainland of Fujian province, became the focal point for crises in 1954 and 1958. We now know that Mao ordered the bombardment of Jinmen for propaganda purposes and as a signal of China's determination rather than as a prelude to invasion.[12] The first bombardment was five days before the signing of the SEATO treaty. The Nationalists replied with airstrikes against the mainland.

Air and sea actions continued in the Taiwan Strait during the first months of 1955. The Nationalists evacuated the most vulnerable of the islands, the Dazhens in February. In return the Nationalists expected the Americans to guarantee the defence of the other islands, Jinmen and Mazu. The actual American commitment was ambiguous. The Formosa resolution passed in both Houses of Congress on 29 January 1955 authorized the President to defend the islands only if he judged an attack on them was an attack on Taiwan itself. Moreover, both the United States and Great Britain held back from committing themselves on the future status of Taiwan. The Senate was reassured that by the Mutual Security Treaty 'the United States does not recognize the sovereignty of the Republic of China over Formosa, even though the treaty expressly lists the island as its territory'. The possibility of 'Two Chinas' was left open theoretically, but the concept has been an anathema to both Nationalists and Communists, who agree that there can only be 'one sun in the heaven'.

In April 1955 the US Secretary of State, Dulles, responding to Zhou Enlai's offer to negotiate at Bandung, admitted somewhat grudgingly, 'I don't think that there occurred any moral or spiritual conversion on the part of the Chinese Communists, but I do think that there may have been a realization of the fact that a real peacefulness, instead of just talk about peace while carrying on a war, was from their standpoint the best policy.'[13] It was agreed (using British diplomatic channels) that direct Sino-American ambassadorial talks should be held. These led to an agreement on the exchange of civilians but virtually nothing else. The talks beginning in Geneva moved to Warsaw in the autumn of 1958 and continued to provide the only direct official contact between the United States and the People's Republic up to 1971. The regular formal meetings were in effect stylized slanging matches with each side stating its position and rebutting the arguments of the other side, (akin to the style adopted at the Korean armistice commission meetings at Panmunjom). Nevertheless, there was the possibility for both sides to signal intentions and to ease tensions at times of crisis. For a time the Chinese appear to have hoped that some progress on the status of Taiwan might be made at the ambassadorial talks and began a letter-writing campaign to high placed officials on Taiwan to convince them that an agreement was in the making.

However, not only was no progress made at the ambassadorial talks, but in June 1957 Dulles appeared to set his face firmly against improving relations with China. Speaking at San Francisco he envisaged that the United States could work towards bringing the Communist regime in China to an end.[14]

For his part Chiang continued to insist on the need for American aid. In May 1957 he got agreement for setting up on Taiwan missiles capable of carrying nuclear or conventional warheads six hundred miles.

SINO-SOVIET DIFFERENCES ON TAIWAN

The PRC and the Soviet Union saw different priorities in the matter of Taiwan. Only a month after the first shelling of the offshore island of Jinmen by the Chinese on 3 September 1954 Soviet leaders Khrushchev and Bulganin visited Beijing to attend the fifth anniversary celebrations of the People's Republic. While the tenor of the meeting with the Chinese leaders was benign, – the visitors agreed to hand back Port Arthur, wind up the joint-stock companies in China's favour and provide a second loan and additional aid for industrial projects – a joint denunciation of the 'American occupation of Taiwan' did not include the offshore islands.

To the Chinese it appeared that the Soviet Union might well sacrifice the 'liberation' of Taiwan for the sake of peace. At the United Nations, the Soviets proposed a resolution which, while calling on the United States to withdraw its forces from Taiwan, stressed the importance of 'an avoidance of hostilities, no matter by whom in the area around Taiwan'.[15] The Chinese were not impressed by Soviet proposals, supported by the British, to solve the dangerous situation 'along the coast of China'. They did not believe that what to them was an internal problem brooking no compromise could be solved by the sort of international intervention which was being proposed. Policy over Taiwan became a persistent point of dissension between China and the USSR.

CHINA AND THE ATOM BOMB

Both the Sino-Soviet alliance and the emergence of the Sino-Soviet rift are related to the policies of the United States. In 1949 the Chinese had seen no alternative to entering the Soviet fold and they were encouraged to remain there by the fact of the atomic bomb. Once the Soviets had become a nuclear power in 1949 they were in a position to counter any American threats to use nuclear weapons against China. Such threats occurred on at least three occasions. Consideration had been given to using nuclear weapons in February and May 1953 to break the deadlock over Korea, and in the winter of 1953–4 to forestall any Chinese intervention in Indochina. The third occasion on which the use of tactical nuclear weapons was postulated was by Eisenhower in March 1955 as a response to 'open armed aggression' by China. Moreover, at one stage of the later Jinmen crisis in 1958 the United States was, according to Eisenhower's memoirs, prepared to use nuclear weapons to defend the island. How seriously should these threats be taken? Whatever we may think in retrospect, at the time the Chinese had to give them due consideration and came up with the published conclusion that the United States was a 'paper tiger'. They also let it be known as early as March 1955 that China, with the biggest population, would be best able to survive a nuclear war.[16]

For all that, the Chinese were far from discounting the importance of nuclear weapons. Indeed in October 1957 the Soviets agreed (according to Mao) to provide China with a 'sample of an atomic bomb and technical data concerning its manufacture'. In the same month the Soviet Sputnik was launched, which in Mao's optimistic view indicated a turning point in international relations in favour of the socialist bloc. When in November Mao attended the world meeting of Communist and Workers' parties held in Moscow he called for the recognition of the leadership of the Soviet Union (appealing in particular to Gomulka of Poland who preferred to emphasize the equality of the countries in the Soviet bloc) in order to present a strong and united front to the United States. There was agreement on the Moscow Declaration, which while upholding the possibility of détente in the Cold War, also recognized that wars in the cause of socialism and against imperialism might be necessary. The text was a skilful blending of the Chinese and Soviet positions.

Not long after the Moscow Declaration Mao delivered his famous speech of 18 November 1957 stating '. . . that the East wind is prevailing over the West wind. That is to say that the forces of socialism are overwhelmingly superior to the forces of imperialism.' He reminded his audience that if, in the event of an atomic war, half the population of the world died, China would come out of it relatively well. If the Soviets already had any qualms about promising Mao assistance to build his own bomb, this speech did not make them feel any better. (Two years later on 20 June 1959 the Soviet Union withdrew assistance for the Chinese nuclear weapons project.)

SINO-SOVIET TENSIONS

The Chinese decided to bombard Jinmen in August 1958. Did they hope to break the deadlock in the Sino-American ambassadorial talks? Were they intending to test the Sino-Soviet alliance? An alarmed Khrushchev flew to Beijing. He complained that Moscow had not been given proper notification of the impending bombardment.[17]

He was also curious why the Chinese had stopped short of occupying the islands. Mao replied 'All we wanted to do was show our potential. We don't want Chiang to be far away from us. . . . Having him on Jinmen and Mazu means we can get him . . . with our shore batteries. . . . If we'd occupied the islands, we would have lost the ability to cause him discomfort any time we want.' When Khrushchev suggested joint naval arrangements to patrol China's coast, Mao assumed these were 'unreasonable demands designed to bring China under military control'.[18]

The unresolved differences came to a head a year later when Khrushchev called in at Beijing on his way back from America. At a banquet in his honour he attacked those who wanted 'to test by force the stability of the capitalist system . . . There are quite realistic possibilities of barring the way to war'.

This warning against adventurism was coupled with a new request for military cooperation. Specifically Khrushchev asked for a wireless station on Chinese soil which would keep in touch with the Soviets' new long range submarines. Mao replied, 'For the last time, no, . . . we don't want you here. We've had the British and other foreigners on our territory for years now, and we're not ever going to let anyone use our land for their own purposes again'.[19]

This Beijing meeting in September 1959 saw the first bitter face-to-face row between Mao and Khrushchev. We have seen that they perceived different priorities on behalf of their respective countries: nevertheless there had been willingness on both sides to maintain the alliance. Who gave up first? It can be argued that Mao set the pace. Was he demanding more support than Khrushchev, with plans for détente with the United States, could give? What support short of war could Mao reasonably expect? After all he himself spoke of keeping the Republic of China on its toes – not invading it. Was Mao asking for a sign, an unambiguous declaration of unequivocal support? If so, there were limits to how far Khrushchev would go along with this. He may well have begun to suspect that Mao was reckless, that he would not object to full-scale war if it served the right ends.

It is also worth asking whether the antagonists were motivated by domestic considerations. It has been suggested that by this time Khrushchev had consolidated his position in the CPSU and no longer needed Chinese support.[20] As for Mao he had to defend his position in the emerging débacle of the Great Leap Forward. In launching the Great Leap, Mao had been attacking Soviet revisionist policies. He had despised the lack of dynamism in domestic affairs and now he was to despair of Soviet commitment to world socialism. On this interpretation the breakdown in relations was because Mao made impossible demands.

In retrospect it is surprising that Western observers seemed to pay so little attention to the impending rift in Sino-Soviet relations. While the sudden Soviet withdrawal of its experts in August 1960 did not go unnoticed, it did not appear to make an immediate impact on American policies towards the USSR and China.

THE SINO-SOVIET SPLIT

At the very time when the practical interests of the two nations had clearly diverged, the dispute appeared to centre on the ideological arena. In April 1960 the Chinese Party launched a major attack on the Soviet Communist Party policy arguing that the line of peaceful coexistence was undermining the forces of revolution throughout the world. In particular they attacked the Soviets for failing to give moral support in China's disputes with India and Indonesia. Paradoxically in neither case was the position of local Communists at stake; indeed in Indonesia China was protesting on behalf of Chinese traders. The fact was that China regarded Asian states as primarily within her sphere of influence and resented Soviet attempts to woo neutralist governments. Khrushchev's tour of south and south-east Asia at the beginning of 1960 added to the disenchantment.

The Chinese succeeded in pressing home their attack on Khrushchev's policies at the meeting of eighty-one Communist parties in Moscow in November 1960. In so far as the final statement was an ingenious concoction of both the Soviet and the Chinese views, observers might have supposed that the cracks had been repaired rather than papered over.

In fact the deep divisions in the extraordinary relationship continued. The Soviet Union was not inclined to help when in the aftermath of the Great Leap Forward China faced famine. It was left to Canada and Australia to ship life-saving supplies of grain to China in 1961. Meanwhile as the Soviet satellites rallied to the side of Moscow, the only support for the Chinese side came from the Albanians. They were punished by the withdrawal of Soviet aid and technicians and were promptly rewarded with Chinese aid and technicians. Thus was established an odd and exclusive relationship between the largest and smallest communist nations. For the next decade white visitors to the People's Republic were liable to be called 'Albanian', a word which became virtually synonymous with 'foreigner' (for many simple Chinese). There were those who hoped to reconcile the antagonists, e.g. the North Vietnamese Communist party which in January 1962 called for a world communist conference to settle differences. Temporarily during the spring of 1962 both Moscow and Beijing appeared to heed this plea and recriminations were toned down in an effort to convince the West that harmony had been restored. Even this appearance of unity was short-lived.

The Soviet Union blamed Beijing for causing unrest on both sides of the Sino-Soviet border when famine prompted tens of thousands to leave Xinjiang for Soviet territory in 1962.[21] China was bitter at the weakness of Soviet support in its border dispute with India which erupted into war in 1962.[22]

Meanwhile Khrushchev was preoccupied with the Cuban missile crisis which became public on 22 October. If the Soviet leader was hoping for Chinese support, he was disappointed. When Khrushchev had to back down and cancel plans for installing missiles on Cuba, Mao saw this capitulation as proof that the Soviet Union under such leadership was not fit to lead the communist bloc.

By now the mutual antagonism was being expressed publicly and explicitly. In January 1963 *Pravda* for the first time openly attacked the Chinese leaders instead of referring to them obliquely as 'dogmatists' or 'leftists' or by attributing their sins to the Albanians. In June 1963 the Chinese spoke out on 'the general line of the international communist movement'. 'Certain persons', Khrushchev and his colleagues, were wrong 'in their attempt to substitute peaceful competition for the revolutionary struggles of the oppressed peoples and nations'.[23] When in July the Chinese attacked the signing of the partial test-ban treaty between the UK, the USA and the USSR as 'a big fraud' which was intended 'to consolidate their nuclear monopoly', the rift was complete.

Was Chinese foreign policy in the early 1960s committed to promoting world revolution? As a general rule it can be asserted that China put her national interests first. Whether at times these interests coincided with those of revolutionaries, and if so whether the Chinese were ideologically rather than pragmatically motivated is worth examination. Certainly Mao himself was never without an ideological banner whether he was using it 'as a hammer . . . to destroy the enemy' in China or in the conviction that world revolution was part of an inevitable process. We have seen that in the dispute with the Soviet Union the Chinese in 1963 began to emphasize the revolutionary struggle of oppressed peoples and moreover to promote themselves as the bearers of the true faith. Instead of pressing for unity within the communist bloc they tried to win other parties to their side. Initially many Asian Communist parties but not that of India joined Beijing while most of the others, but not Albania's, joined Moscow.

INTERPRETING THE SINO-SOVIET RIFT

How far back can we trace the origin of the Sino-Soviet rift in the light of the latest available documentation? In 1963 when the breach was publicly acknowledged in the polemics from both sides, the Chinese said the differences between China and the Soviet Union began with the Twentieth Congress of the CPSU in 1956, when Khrushchev criticized Stalin (see Chapter 3). However, the known history of relations between the CPSU and the CCP from its early days was enough to suggest that this was an oversimplification which omitted decades of perceived different interests; recent publications in China and Russia now provide documentation to show that disenchantment between the two parties went back a long way.

In the late 1960s and early 1970s the predominant line of interpretation in the West, replacing the 'monolithic communism' theory, was that deep distrust between Mao and Stalin originated in the 1930s. There is disagreement about how far this should now be modified in the light of recently published CCP materials. Michael Sheng, for example, has come to the conclusion that 'in the period 1935–50 . . . relations were much more harmonious than we have ever imagined. Stalin and Mao were revolutionary comrades rather than adversaries despite their own 'personality cults'.[24]

The evidence of witnesses to Mao's visit to Moscow in 1950 is contradictory. The two interpreters recollect that the overall relationship between the two leaders was courteous and even cordial, while Stalin's personal envoy, Ivan Kovalov, agrees with Khrushchev that Mao was 'very upset'. Khrushchev was writing more than fifteen years later, the other about forty years later. What of Mao's own recollections? A recently declassified report of Mao's conversation with the Soviet ambassador in March 1956 has Mao speaking bitterly about insulting treatment.[25]

What was Mao's general opinion of Stalin in the long term? In conversation with a Yugoslav delegation in September 1956 Mao recalled: (1) Stalin was responsible for the Wang Ming line (as promoted by the Moscow trained group at Yanan) which 'ended up destroying ninety per cent of our strength in our bases'; (2) in the anti-Japanese war Stalin, through Wang Ming, advocated collaboration with the GMD to the extent of 'giving up our Party's own armed force'; (3) at Yalta Stalin with Roosevelt and Churchill handed over the whole of China to Chiang Kai-shek while giving hardly any 'material and moral support especially moral support to us'; (4) Mao complained that Stalin suspected him of being a 'half-hearted Tito', a tag which was removed only when China stood up to America in Korea. However, the Chinese people had been kept in the dark about this: 'only our Central Committee was aware that Stalin blocked our revolution and regarded me as a half-hearted Tito'.[26] In spite of his frustration and anger Mao believed it was necessary to support the Soviet Union as the leader of world communism and for the same reason did not make a public fuss about Khrushchev's denunciation of Stalin. In fact the Chinese ambassador to Moscow, Liu says that Khrushchev sought Mao's support during the post-Stalin succession struggle.[27] He suggests Mao may well have expected some quid pro quo.

The early origins of the Sino-Soviet rift have been obscured because both sides – but particularly Mao – chose to overlook differences in the hope of eventual gains. When that hope faded there was little to stop the rift widening irrevocably.

5 The Great Leap Forward, 1956–64

'I am a complete outsider when it comes to economic construction. I understand nothing about industrial planning . . . comrades, in 1958 and 1959 the main responsibility was mine.'

Mao, at Lushan Conference, August 1959

The Great Leap Forward 1958–9 was in part a response to the inadequacy of Soviet Aid and the perceived inappropriateness of the Soviet model in China. Mao advocated an alternative way forward, mobilizing China's human resources, combining local initiative with the spirit of self-sacrifice and self-sufficiency in a new community structure. Thus the achievement of socialism would be speeded up, rural China organized into self-reliant commune units, the peasants forged into a truly revolutionary corps while at the same time industry would be diversified.

Mao was the driving force behind this scheme. It failed. Mao, sidelined as a result, could be said 'to have learned nothing and forgotten nothing'. The Great Leap was to lead to an even greater upheaval – the Cultural Revolution.

ORIGINS

In January 1956 a book was published in Beijing with a preface by Mao Zedong, explaining that it was 'a collection of material intended for people working in the countryside'. It had been in preparation for some months and out of 176 articles 44 had been selected to be published in an abridged edition of 270,000 words. It is a classic exposition of the Chairman's belief in the maxim 'From the people to the people.' Mao had sent investigators into the countryside. Members of his own bodyguard were ordered to visit their home villages and report back. The reprinted reports, each bearing an editorial note, were presented in this book to show the successful implementation of the semi-socialist agricultural producers co-operatives. In Mao's words it proved that '. . . we need only one year – 1956 – to practically complete the changeover to semi-socialist co-operation in agriculture.' He added that in another three or four years 'by 1959 or 1960' the transformation would be made to fully socialist co-operatives (collectives). Mao himself wrote a short preface to each article bubbling with enthusiasm for the success of the peasants, particularly the poor and lower middle classes. He noted the importance of those with some education taking the lead.

'All people who have some education ought to be very happy to work in the countryside if they get the chance. In our vast rural areas there is plenty of room for them to develop their talents to the full'.[1] He also criticized those comrades who had produced articles heavy with party jargon. 'How many years will it be before we see a little less of that party jargon which gives us such a headache'.

At this time Mao had prepared and presented a draft for a Twelve-Year Programme for agriculture. This included a scheme for water conservation on a large scale and envisaged significant increases in both grain and cotton production. Included in the plan was an appeal to eliminate four pests: mosquitoes, flies, rats and sparrows. A nationwide campaign was pursued enthusiastically to the point when it was discovered that without sparrows to keep them in check the insect populations knew no bounds.

Mao's outline scheme received initial approval by the Central Committee in January 1956. Mao later complained that this acceptance was half-hearted and the programme was in effect shelved pending further argument. Throughout 1956 these ideas were tied up with the whole question of the role of the intellectuals. Serious doubts about collectivization, coinciding with the Hundred Flowers movement, were not resolved until October 1957 when the Central Committee gave the go-ahead to Mao's radical Twelve-Year Plan. Mao was in the ascendant. The second Five-Year Plan, now suspect as too closely linked to the development of heavy industry in the Soviet mode, was put aside, the material incentives introduced in wage-reform measures in early 1956 were denounced and in November a new wage policy stressed moral and social incentives. In retrospect it is remarkable that Mao was able to launch the Great Leap Forward.[2] Since this was against the considered advice of many at least as well informed as Mao and since it led to almost immediate disaster, one wonders why he was allowed to get away with it. The fact was that many in the leadership appear to have believed at that time in the heroic way forward. Partly this arose out of the perceived drawbacks of Soviet style economics in the Chinese context. It was also a response to the disappointing achievements of the first Five-Year Plan. It was a reaffirmation of the Yanan way; Mao's answer to the critics and the doubters was 'Walking on two legs' – agriculture and industry would go hand in hand in the countryside. Using her own resources with the maximum mobilization of human effort China would, in fifteen years, surpass Great Britain in industrial development. There was to be a nationwide transformation to a new economic and political framework for society. The villages were too small as units of resource. Planning could best be done at the level of what had formerly been the *xiang*. In imperial China this was an administrative grouping comprising a number of villages with a population from 20,000 up to 50,000. It was now called a commune, with deliberate overtones of the Paris commune of 1871.[3]

The new economic collectives were at first organized at the village or team level but local independence was soon subsumed within the larger communes. The whole population was mobilized to develop not only agriculture and new local industrial enterprises but also (where and as appropriate) to take part in large tasks such as water conservation and land reclamation. Propaganda stressed mass line principles of persuasion; living and working together the peasants would be forged into a revolutionary corps. The family appeared redundant; cooking was to give way to mess halls, children were to be looked after in crèches, thus liberating mothers to work in the fields and stoke the fires of improvised iron furnaces. There were those not only in China but among western observers who saw in the Communes the realization of the socialist goal – communism. As rations were doled out in lieu of earnings they believed that 'to each according to his work' had become 'to each according to his needs'.

THE GREAT LEAP 1958–9: TRIUMPH OF THREE RED BANNERS

During the first stage of the Great Leap Forward from autumn 1957 to spring 1958 the peasants were mobilized in military style, reminiscent of Yanan days, for large scale public works. This led to a shortage of labour for the spring planting. The second Five-Year Plan had been due to start in January 1958 designed to achieve an increase in industrial production of around 14 per cent. Instead new and much more ambitious targets were now envisaged.

It was during the second session of the CCP's Eighth Congress in May 1958 that the programme for the People's Communes was officially endorsed. The first commune, established in Henan province in July, was called 'Sputnik Commune'. In August 1958 the Politburo formally approved the communes and stated 'it seems that the attainment of Communism in China is no longer a remote future event.'[4] By the end of the year 740,000 production co-operatives had been reorganized into 26,000 communes.

The educational aspect of the Great Leap reflected Mao's yearning for the revival of the Yanan tradition. In January 1958 he promoted a 'work and study' curriculum which down-graded the bookish, rote-learning methods of the traditionalists. For peasants and workers there was to be better access to primary schooling and also to the middle schools and universities.

The decision that people all over China (an estimated 90 million) should try their hand at making steel was set in train in the autumn of 1958. The idea was to double steel production to 10.7 million tons in the first year and increase it to 30 million tons in 1959 and 60 million tons in 1960. These targets were not related to the availability of iron ore, coal and transport. To supply over 600,000 'backyard' furnaces, metal of all sorts was melted down. Woodlands were cut down for fuel. Even by autumn 1958 impressive achievements were being reported by the cadres who were professionally bound to produce results which met the targets set. The boundless enthusiasm of the participants was also remarked on by foreigners.[5]

As it happened, the weather conditions in 1958 contributed to the production of a good crop of grain; 200–210 million tons compared with the 375 million tons which was announced by the central authorities. The Sixth Plenum of the Central Committee, meeting from 28 November to 10 December, endorsed inflated figures not only for grain but also for cotton, up from 1.6 million to 3.3 million tons, coal from 130 million to 270 million tons, and steel from 5.3 million to 11 million tons.[6] The planners were thus encouraged to set even higher targets for 1959. In fact grain production fell in 1959 to between 160 and 170 million tons.

Propaganda stoked up and reflected the general euphoria in the summer and autumn of 1958. As the inflated production figures rolled in, posters and loudspeakers proclaimed the triumph of the 'Three Red Banners' – the General Line, the Great Leap Forward, and the People's Communes.

The high heady days were soon over. In a matter of months it was clear that all was not as it seemed. However, the ideological vested

Figure 5.1 Agricultural production propaganda. The density of the crop apparently supports the children in this photograph from *China Pictorial*, no. 99, 1958.

interest was too great for a sudden and immediate renunciation of the policies. Many meetings and conferences were held in the first half of 1959 to examine the problems created by trying to go too far, too quickly. The general consensus was that a period of retrenchment could be followed by further advances.

Of all the problems coming to light the most serious was the fiasco of grain production. Mao had long been impressed by the theories of Lysenko that genetic miracles could be performed. The farce played out in China involved such sleight of hand as replanting grain in thicker rows on the days of Mao's visit and photographing children on hidden benches as if they were supported by the density of the crop. More seriously it involved every one eating so much in 1958 that the granaries were depleted. It was politically correct to overeat; William Hinton, the American author of *Shenfan*, reported the words of a peasant: 'We ate a lot of meat. It was considered revolutionary to eat meat. If you didn't eat meat it wouldn't do.'[7]

Having exaggerated the harvests the rural cadres had to meet increasing demands for food quotas going to the cities; grain exports were stepped up by 50 per cent to the Soviet Union while free grain was shipped to the friendly nations, North Korea, North Vietnam and Albania.

MAO CHALLENGED BY PENG DEHUAI

Mao's standing and authority was to be challenged at the Central Committee meeting at Lushan in July 1959. By then Mao had already relinquished the post of Head of State to Liu Shaoqi in April. In spite of the timing he was not, as has sometimes been suggested, forced to resign this largely ceremonial post; he had announced in December 1958 that he did not intend to stand for re-election. It was however, at a meeting of the Politburo in April 1959 that Peng Dehuai,[8] the Minister of Defence, criticized Mao's leadership. He blamed him for 'personally taking command' from as far back as Yanan in 1942.[9]

As Minister of Defence Peng did not eagerly step into the role of economic critic, but he could not avoid noticing ominous signs. At first he had pointed enthusiastically to the backyard furnaces, for example in October 1958 visiting the north-west province of Gansu, but was soon disillusioned when he found that agricultural as well as military activities had been suspended and that houses and fruit trees had been burnt to produce useless metal. However, at the Wuchang conference and plenum in November–December 1958 he voiced only minor criticisms about the more extreme grain forecasts and in fact accepted the published figure for 1958, 375 million tons.

When in 1959 Peng visited his home village Niaoshi in Hunan (which happened to be very close to Mao's Shaoshan) he faced the impending reality of man-made disaster. Visiting the hungry old folks at the Niaoshi Happiness Home, Peng himself spoke of the 'deception' of exaggerated yields. When he asked the provincial party secretary for his opinion of the steel production campaign, the man first replied non-committally that it was difficult to say and then, at Peng's request, agreed to send out a provincial directive against the exaggerating tendencies of the Great Leap. In return Peng said that he would let Mao know what was going on, so implying that the Chairman's policies rather than being fundamentally faulty had been misapplied.

Before he left his home province Peng wrote a poem.

The millet is scattered all over the ground,
The leaves of the sweet potatoes are withered,
The young and the strong have gone to melt iron,
To harvest the grain there are children and old women.
How shall we get through next year?
I shall agitate and speak out on behalf of the People.[10]

In fact Peng did not speak out on the economic issue at that time: making only the allusions noted above to Mao's leadership style. He then left on a visit to the Soviet Union and Eastern Europe from 24 April to 13 June. It was later said that he informed 'bald-headed Khrushchev' of the shortcomings of the Great Leap Forward. When he returned he asked to be excused from attending the Lushan meeting.

While he was away the leadership had learned how greatly the figures for grain production had been exaggerated, and by the end of June it was clear that the 1959 harvest would not be good: in the north-east there had been a long dry spell, in parts of the south there had been flooding.

In June Mao went to his home village at Shaoshan for the first time in thirty-two years before he went on to the Central Committee meeting at Lushan. Peng Dehuai was present: he would have preferred the chief of staff Huang Kecheng to take his place, but Mao had phoned to ask him to be there. The stage was set. Peng, noting that both he and Mao had visited the same commune in Shaoshan said; 'I asked the Chairman what was his finding. He said that he had not talked about the matter. In my opinion he had'. Apart from this suggestion that Mao was lying, Peng behaved quite correctly. He wrote and circulated a letter in which criticisms of the Great Leap were moderately expressed and he refrained from putting the blame on Mao personally. Coincidentally about this time an article critical of the Great Leap appeared in *Pravda* written by Nikita Khrushchev.

Others at Lushan agreed with Peng. Mao, while admitting many mistakes, chose to see the criticisms as a challenge which threatened Party unity and which was being made in collusion with the Soviets. He successfully played the patriotic card. And he narrowed the debate into a choice between himself and Peng Dehuai. 'If you have caught me in the wrong, you can punish me', he said. But he also warned 'If you the Liberation Army don't want to follow me, I will seek out a Red army', and again 'If the Chinese People's Liberation army should follow Peng Dehuai, I will go to fight guerrilla war.[11]

There were some bitter recriminations replete with coarse language. But the conference swung into line behind Mao, not only in the cause of unity, but probably fearing for their own positions if the assessment of blame were to permeate through the whole Politburo. They saw that Peng had gone too far. He saw that he had been outployed. Peng became visibly depressed; the doctor thought he was ill but Peng knew better. He wrote to Mao in September 'I now fully realise that my bourgeois world outlook and methodology were deep-rooted and my individualism most serious . . . I have been unworthy of your teaching and patience with me for the past thirty years. I am filled with indescribable shame and remorse'.[12] Peng volunteered to rehabilitate himself by working as a peasant but he was sent to run a state farm in Heilongjiang.

He made an unsuccessful attempt at a political comeback in 1962. Arrested during the Cultural Revolution, he died in detention in 1974. He was rehabilitated posthumously in 1978 (Chapter 8). In 1996 his career was celebrated officially at a top level gathering to mark the publication of a biography.

THE THREE BAD YEARS, 1959–61: ABANDONING THE GREAT LEAP

There were crises on more than one front in the three years from 1959. Shortages of food and materials were nationwide and were recognized. In Beijing the children of the highest party officials were exhorted to be frugal. Less publicized at the time was the fact that in certain regions there was famine, now reckoned to have accounted for 20 million deaths, leading to sporadic outbursts of cannibalism.[13] Moreover drought, typhoons and flooding contributed to the devastation of half of the cultivatable area notably in Hebei, Henan, Shandong and Shanxi.

Certainly the extent of the disaster was not revealed at the time. It is instructive to see how the premier Zhou Enlai reacted to the situation in the late summer of 1959. He was as aware as anyone at the Lushan meeting of the real state of affairs. Having asked party provincial secretaries 'for actual figures, not percentages', he presented a memo to the conference showing that the balance between finances, resources and production had been totally upset in 1958.[14] Nevertheless he endeavoured to save face for Mao and presumably for himself when on 26 August he addressed the Standing Committee of the NPC emphasizing the need for 'adjusting' targets while defending the principle of mass participation in iron and steel production. He made a point of defending the community dining rooms – 'they suit the requirements of the masses and therefore are welcomed by them . . . especially . . . working women . . . because they relieve them to a great extent of heavy household chores and facilitate their taking part in production like their menfolk.[15] In short Zhou made a thorough criticism of overambitious targets while reaffirming the principles of the Great leap, the mobilization of the masses and 'walking on two legs.'

To what extent was the disaster man-made, the result of Mao's policies, or was it caused at least in part by natural disasters? At the time there was much talk of bad weather conditions and sympathetic western commentators emphasized natural rather than man-made causes. The evidence is far from clear. Some meteorologists have confirmed that the 1959–60 drought was the worst since 1877[16] but there is contradictory evidence. Only in recent years has the full extent of the great famine been recognized and the generally agreed view of Chinese and foreign observers been to condemn the Great Leap unequivocally. There is still some debate: for example Jack Gray writing in 1990, cites Liu Shaoqi who said that the disasters were 70 per cent 'man-made' and points out that 'the left denied this'. Gray credits Mao with having faced up to the fact of the famine and given orders to deal with it.[17]

There are also those who argue that it was not a complete failure in the long term. Methods of flood control and irrigation using intensive labour which were developed in 1957–8 have since been put to good effect. The diversification of economic enterprise in the countryside was successfully revived later. Even the much ridiculed backyard blast furnaces became profitable enterprises in the rural economies of the 1980s.[18]

The Great Leap was not publicly condemned at the time; nor indeed was it officially and explicitly brought to an end. Even allowing for the fact that, as Mao later complained, the Leadership was preoccupied with the Soviet relationship it is notable that internal politics remained high on the agenda. In the aftermath of the Lushan meeting Mao was fighting back by purging the 'right opportunists'.[19] Thus in late 1959 there was an attempt to revive the Great Leap accompanied by the rounding-up of 'rightist' peasants; they were put in prison where many died in the ensuing starvation.

However, by 1960 any thought of reviving the Great Leap was being abandoned. The movement was brought to an end by economic realities. While lip-service continued to be paid to Mao and the Three Red Banners, between July and November 1960 the Central Committee issued guidelines for a new policy. The commune as an administrative unit was reduced in size; the number of communes increased from 26,000 to 74,000. Responsibilities were shifted back from the commune to brigade and team level. Eventually the team became the unit of accounting. Thus the peasants were reassured of their place within the local village-sized unit.

Perhaps most encouraging for the peasants was the restoration of their private plots, taken away in 1953, restored in 1954, taken again in 1957/58 and restored in 1962. There they could grow a few vegetables and even engage in a little private marketing, but such changes did not come in time to forestall grievances leading to armed revolt in at least two provinces, Honan and Shandong. In 1962 refugees from Guangdong fled to Hong Kong while from Xinjiang some crossed over to the Soviet Union adding a little local tension to the deteriorating relationship (see Chapter 4).

MAO ON THE SIDELINES

Peng's downfall and his replacement as Minister of Defence by Lin Biao did not mean his ideas had been repudiated. On the contrary the leading members of the Politburo who stopped short of publicly undermining the position of the Chairman did so not only because of their strong residue of respect, but also because it would have served no purpose in the economic and diplomatic crises facing China. In effect Mao's influence was being put to one side. He complained that he was treated like a dead ancestor.

As policies in the hard-hit rural sector veered to the right with the restoration of incentives and private plots, Mao saw his vision of revolution in the countryside fading. Worse, there was evidence of corruption among rural cadres. But Mao and a faction supporting him were not lying down. The 1962 socialist education campaign was originally intended to restore collectivization. Mao drafted a resolution in February 1963, the 'Early Ten Points', proposing that work teams should mobilize the masses to criticize bad party cadres. In autumn 1963 this resolution was revised by Deng Xiaoping as the 'Later Ten Points', which said there should be a minimum of disruption and certainly no attack on the middle peasants. By June 1964 Mao was arguing that bad cadres should be dealt with locally by the masses (poorer peasants), who knew them, and thus reformed rather than removed by higher authority.

Then in September 1964 Liu Shaoqi produced the 'Revised Later Ten Points'. This had been influenced by the field work of Liu's wife, Wang Guangmei, who had gone incognito to the countryside and found horrifying evidence of corruption, compounded by collusion between village cadres and higher party officials. It was proposed that the poor peasant leagues backed by militia should be so organized at commune level that they could withstand the cadres. Later it was charged against Liu that this was 'left in form but right in essence'. To Mao an approach directed only against the cadres and which did not attack 'capitalist roaders' amongst the peasantry was flawed. Moreover, Mao believed that the large work teams sent down would in practice override the poor peasant leagues.

In January 1965 Mao produced what was to be known as the Twenty-three Articles calling for an alliance of peasants, cadres and work-teams. The attack was not only on individual enterprise in rural activities and on corruption; Mao insisted that reform was needed at all levels – up to the Central Committee itself! The lines had been drawn for a battle royal.

6 The Cultural Revolution, 1965–71

The Great Proletarian Cultural Revolution was probably the most extraordinary political upheaval in the twentieth century. In contrast to the economic and social upheaval of the Great Leap Forward the Cultural Revolution was essentially political. It centred on Mao and his ambitions; concerning both his personal power and his revolutionary ideals. To achieve the latter he had to overcome his opponents in the Party leadership.

Mao saw that his role as leader was to turn China away from the revisionist road. It was a question of maintaining faith in the future of egalitarian socialism. Something had to be done to counter those such as Liu Shaoqi, who had been watering down Mao's revolutionary proposals (see Chapter 5) and Deng Xiaoping who had cynically remarked that it didn't matter what colour the cat was as long as it caught mice.

The struggle within the leadership spread to the universities in May 1966 and to the workers at the end of 1966. Mao unleashed forces which could not easily be controlled, even by himself. The most dramatic period, characterized by Red Guards waving Little Red Books and shouting Maoist slogans, was 1966–8. By 1969, the Red Guards had been curbed and the Cultural Revolution was said to be over, but later historians have suggested that it lasted until Mao's death in 1976. The timing is thus linked to the interpretation.

Questions which arise are: (1) was the Cultural Revolution primarily a struggle for power between Mao and his opponents, or was Mao genuinely committed to reversing the evolution of a new self-interested bureaucratic class and the trend since the Great Leap to dilute socialism? (2) How far was the Cultural Revolution a genuinely popular movement inspired at the grass roots, or was it almost wholly manipulated by elements of the leadership? (3) How do we explain the fervour of mass participation, the intergroup struggles and the violence?

HOW DID IT BEGIN?

There is no doubt that it arose out of the disagreements which Mao was having with his colleagues in the aftermath of the Great Leap Forward. Mao was suspicious and resentful of the Party leaders and bureaucrats, who while giving him the respect due to a dead ancestor, were making revisionist inroads into his ideal of a revolutionary state on the road to communism. The socialist education campaigns were intended both to remove corruption and to restore the mass line politics of collectivization. Mao crystallized his position in the 23 articles, January 1965. (Chapter 5)

By 1965, notwithstanding the debates within the leadership, China had largely recovered from the economic effects of the Great Leap Forward. Agricultural production had made a good recovery, up to 1957 levels, light industry was expanding at the rate of 27 per cent a year and heavy industry at 17 per cent. By the mid-1960s output in heavy and light industry and consumer goods was double that in 1957.[1] The mobilization of labour for irrigation projects and land clearance during the Great Leap had made more productive land available. Some peasants acknowledged that they were now reaping the benefits of this policy.[2]

Mao's proclaimed model for industry, the Daqing oilfield in Heilongjiang, had struck rich deposits, boosting oil production tenfold since 1957. China was freed from dependence on the Soviet union and the supply of natural gas was up fortyfold. It was a very considerable achievement, but there was some comment by critics that because it had used foreign equipment and technology, it had not been such an uncompromising model of Maoist self-reliance as it was portrayed.

A similar grand example for agriculture was the Learn from Dazhai campaign launched in 1964. Dazhai was a production brigade in a poor mountainous commune in Xiyang county, Shanxi, where it was claimed that production had increased fivefold by using mass mobilization. In late 1964 a team of investigators reported that the claims for Dazhai were based on false and misleading figures at the very time that Chen Yonggui, the brigade leader, was receiving the highest accolade from Zhou Enlai and meeting with Mao Zedong. More was at stake than the reliability of statistical information. Those who said 'There are woodworms in the staff of the red banner of Dazhai'[3] were attacking Chairman Mao.

Contemporaneous with the Learn from Dazhai campaign in 1964 was the Third Front programme to build heavy industry inland away from areas vulnerable to attack.[4] Shrouded in military secrecy, its importance during the years of the Cultural Revolution has only recently been assessed (with new data).In Mao's mind the mobilization of resources for dealing with the threat of attack from abroad went hand in hand with the need to expose the internal enemies – revisionists who, like Khrushchev, were following the capitalist road.

Meanwhile Lin Biao, who had been appointed to succeed Peng Dehuai as Minister of Defence in 1959, was emerging as a loyal acolyte of Mao. He compiled a breviary of Mao's writings as a pocketbook for the troops (May 1964) later dubbed the Little Red Book. The army was to become the incarnation of Maoism. In 1965 the officers' uniform was modified to signify egalitarianism. The visible difference was that officers jackets had four pockets, the soldiers only two. Then on 3 September Lin published a long article, 'Long Live the Victory of People's War'. On the one hand it was a statement on foreign policy: no involvement in Vietnam, no compromise with the Soviet Union (see Chapter 7). It was also conveniently timed as a declaration of ongoing revolution inside China.

If Mao's role in the run-up to the Cultural Revolution had been attempting to defend his policies, he was also getting ready to take the offensive. Liu Shaoqi, Mao's likely successor, had failed to respond favourably to Mao's 23 articles, January 1965. Well known as supporters of Liu were Beijing officials Wu Han and Deng Tuo, respectively Vice Mayor and one of the Party secretaries of the city government under the mayor Peng Zhen. Deng, a poet and columnist, and Wu, an eminent historian and popular playwright, had both attacked Mao satirically. Deng had enjoyed himself making fun of Mao as an unreliable man who wrote childish verse; Wu Han's play 'Hai Jui dismissed from office' likened Mao's treatment of Peng Dehuai to a Ming emperor's high-handed treatment of an honest official. It was time to bring Wu Han to task. At the September 1965 Politburo meeting Mao urged that he be criticized and, cunningly, Peng Zhen was put in charge as head of a five-person group looking into cultural reform. However, the self-confident mayor avoided taking action. Mao complained that Peng's control of Beijing was so complete that there was no room even to put in a needle. On 10 November 1965 in Shanghai under the guidance of Mao's wife Jiang Qing[5], the radical writer Yao Wenyuan published an article criticizing Wu Han. This was later said to be the 'first bugle call' of the Cultural Revolution.[6]

At first Peng Zhen chose to defend Wu Han but Mao followed up his attack. In a speech to a party conference in Hangzhou, attended by Peng Zhen, Mao condemned revisionism in science and culture. He explained how he had instructed his own daughter. 'I said to my own child, "You go down to the countryside and tell the poor and lower-middle peasants, my dad says that after studying a few years we became more and more stupid. Please . . . be my teachers. I want to learn from you.'"7

If Mao was using the cultural debate as an excuse to launch a campaign against his political opponents, he was certainly successful. People began to distance themselves from those who were perceived as Mao's enemies; Deng Xiaoping stopped playing bridge with Wu Han. Hoping to resolve the matter, Peng's Five-Person Group drew up a statement, the February Outline Report, which considered whether 'people like Wu Han' should be treated as political problems to be suppressed as necessary, or whether they should be reasoned with on the principle of 'seeking the truth from facts'. This latter solution was favoured by the Five-Person Group, and approved by the Politburo. Peng Zhen apparently hoped that Mao would accept this as a compromise; in some anxiety he travelled down to see Mao, who was in Wuhan, and asked him to approve the February Outline Report, but Mao was obdurate. He refused to read or comment on it. Mao's wife Jiang Qing was asked by Lin Biao to set up 'A forum on work in literature and art for the armed forces'. This promptly rejected the February Report, stressed the importance of class struggle and called for a 'Great Socialist Cultural Revolution.'

TO OCTOBER 1966: 'BOMBARD THE HEADQUARTERS'

Mao called a meeting of the Standing Committee of the Politburo which met from 17 to 20 March 1966, followed by a Central Committee work conference, and to both he drummed out the theme that it was time for local authorities to rebel against the centre. The Five-Person Group (which had shown itself in the February Report to be ready to compromise) was replaced by a new body – the Cultural Revolution Group consisting of Mao's supporters, who at this time included his wife Jiang Qing, Yao Wenyuan who had written the attack on Wu Han's play, and Chen Boda, Senior Party member in the Chinese Academy of Sciences, formerly Mao's secretary. Key figures who apparently knew better than to stand up to Mao were Liu Shaoqi, Deng Xiaoping and Zhou Enlai, who joined in bringing about the dismissal of Peng Zhen.

Important decisions were made at an enlarged meeting of the Politburo between 4 and 18 May. Lin Biao spoke, he accused Peng Zhen and others of planning a military coup. Accordingly troops loyal to

Mao had been sent to key installations in Beijing. An extensive debate over many days led to the May 16th circular, which emphasized the threat from counter-revolutionary elements who had 'sneaked into the Party, the Government, the army and various cultural circles'. From this a thinly veiled attack was developed on 'top party people in authority who were taking the capitalist road'. Eventually it was to be understood that the chief villain was China's Khrushchev, none other than Liu Shaoqi himself. For the moment Liu was not named; he was in the unenviable position of being pressed to act against revisionism while being responsible for maintaining the central control of the Party. With Mao continuing to operate from central China, Liu was conspicuously in charge in the capital. Throughout June and into July Liu tried to wrestle with this dilemma. To add to the ambiguity of his position there was a growing question mark over his future as Mao's chosen successor.

Meanwhile the universities became involved, with some lecturers and students responding dramatically to the May 16th circular. They were encouraged by Mao's appeals to the young, and by visiting representatives of the Cultural Revolution Group who were sent to drum up support.[8] At Beijing University a young female lecturer in the philosophy department, who had long been in disagreement with the head of the Party at the university, put up a wall newspaper criticizing the Party administration. When the Youth League was ordered to suppress the poster, Mao had it published in the *People's Daily*. Desperately hoping to uphold the role of the Party, maintain his own position, and control the burgeoning unrest, Liu Shaoqi sent work teams into the universities and colleges throughout the country (a method of control which had been used before, for example, during the Socialist Education Movement). Backed by Liu Shaoqi the work teams laid down rules of behaviour, forbade the writing of wall newspapers and street demonstrations and distinguished between party and non-party matters.

Student reaction to the work teams fell into two categories. Those who supported the work teams were likely to be the children of party functionaries and those who could claim to be in the acceptable category of worker/peasant. They were opposed by those of 'bourgeois' origin who were happy to protest against the entrenched positions of the bureaucracy and the cadre-class. Thus emerged two groups of Red Guards as they came to be called (Mao used the term for first time in a letter of 1 August) sometimes distinguished (in the West) as moderates versus the radicals.

Mao was clearly playing a daring, indeed reckless role. Lest anyone should think he was not up to it physically at the age of 72, he went for a public swim in the Yangzi on 16 July. With 5,000 young swimmers in attendance, he was said to have covered nine miles in 65 minutes, going downstream.[9] Then he called a meeting for early August of the Central Committee Plenum, the first since 1962, and, excluding some potential opponents, brought in some known radicals and PLA men. On 5 August, on the door of the room where the Central Committee met, he put up his own poster 'Bombard the headquarters'. Subsequently published in schools and universities, the gist of its message, less dramatic than the headline, was explicit criticism of the activity of the work teams. Implicitly it called on the radicals to attack the Head of State Liu Shaoqi himself. But, in fact, so far from opposing Mao's call for educational reforms, which included changing the admission criteria, Liu's work teams had done some pretty thorough purging. For example, in Qinghua University a team led by Liu's wife had demanded self-criticism from all party cadres with the result that 70 per cent were sent to labour camps.[10] But Mao saw this as irrelevant window-dressing designed to keep the Party in control and its top leaders above criticism.

It was a victory for the radical students, at first in a small minority, when the work teams were withdrawn, and the Youth League, which had been monopolized by cadres' children and those of good (i.e. worker/peasant) background, suspended its activities. However, a moderate wing of the Red Guards continued to support the Party and encouraged diversionary attacks on 'bourgeois intellectuals'.

On 8 August the Central Committee adopted a 'sixteen-point decision' which was intended to provide guidelines and keep the revolution under control. It began:

> The Great Proletarian Cultural Revolution now unfolding is a great revolution that touches people to their very souls and constitutes a new stage in the development of the socialist revolution in our country . . . Large numbers of revolutionary young people . . . have become courageous and daring path-breakers . . . Through the media of big-character posters and great debates, they argue things out, expose and criticize thoroughly and launch resolute attacks on the open and hidden representatives of the bourgeoisie . . . The cultural revolutionary groups . . . are something new and . . . are an excellent bridge to keep our Party in close contact with the masses.[11]

The resolution went on to propose that the groups should become standing organizations with a 'system of general elections like that of the Paris Commune'.[12] Was it really envisaged that some kind of mass participatory democracy under the Party was about to evolve?

On 18 August Mao, with Lin Biao at his side, took the stand in Tiananmen Square wearing a Red Guard armband at a mass rally of a million young people. Schools and colleges were closed during the summer and students were being encouraged to travel about the country. As Mao said '. . . the trains are free now, are they not'? In the months to come millions made the pilgrimage to successive rallies in Beijing or travelled to other provinces to 'exchange experiences'. These were heady days for millions of young people, many of whom were seeing other parts of the country for the first time in their lives. With all the exuberance went political harangue, and denunciation of revisionists, bourgeois reactionaries and class enemies. Bands of Red Guards set out to destroy the 'Four olds': old thought, old culture, old customs, old habits, to which was added anything considered Western or foreign or decadent, for example Beethoven's music. The furore mounted, groups of Red Guards fought one another. They also turned their fury on 'capitalist roaders', including intellectuals. Anyone unfortunate enough to be denounced was liable to be physically abused and even driven to suicide. For a time Mao was tolerant of the youngsters' excesses. Mao himself was riding the crest of a wave. At a work conference in October both Liu Shaoqi and Deng Xiaoping confessed their errors.[13] A few days later Mao took the microphone at a mass rally and on the only occasion in the Cultural Revolution when he addressed the Red Guards face to face said 'You must let politics take command, go to the masses, and be with the masses. You must conduct the Great Proletarian Cultural Revolution even better'.[14]

FROM OCTOBER 1966: 'THERE WILL STILL ALWAYS BE HEADS'

In winter 1966–7 the workers also became involved, notably in Shanghai but in other cities as well. The contending factions were the radical Red Rebels, whose attack was focused largely on the official trade unions, and the Scarlet Guards who defended the trade unions and the Party. These 'conservatives' pressed with some success for higher wages and better conditions for certain groups of industrial workers.

When in November Zhang Chunqiao, member of the Cultural Revolution Group and ally of Jiang Qing, arrived in Shanghai from Beijing he urged the radical rebels in the name of Mao to take over the government of the city. They were opposed by the Scarlet Guards. Moreover, the situation was complicated by the fact that there were seven hundred rebel organizations! A so-called 'Shanghai Paris Commune'[15] was created to govern the city and, it was hoped, unite the many political factions under a radical banner. The idea was imitated in many cities throughout China. This was in line with the mass political involvement envisaged in the sixteen points directive, but it was doomed. First, the relatively highly skilled workers of Shanghai were inclined to support the Scarlet Guards and not the other groups. Second, setting up an elected 'Commune' threatened the very existence of the Party, indeed the erstwhile leaders of the Communist Party in Shanghai were in jail and third, Mao himself saw fit to condemn extreme anarchism. He noted that the demand to do away with the leaders of society was unrealistic and anarchic. 'In reality there will still always be "Heads"'[16]

The political chaos was compounded by the fact that the warring factions claimed to be leftists following Mao's leadership. When Mao turned to the army (14 January 1967) both to restore order and to support the left-wing groups he told them to restrict the power of the Party machine. This was not so easily done. Provincial party leaders organized their own Red Guard groups to fight the original Maoist Red Guards and, authorizing bonuses, persuaded the workers to endorse them as genuine leaders of the left.

One initiative to calm the radical tide was made in February 1967 when the Cultural Revolution Group[17] were challenged by senior members of the civil and military establishment such as Zhu De, Chen Yun, Chen Yi, and others. They were full of scorn for the chaotic state of affairs which had developed under Mao and Lin Biao and took the opportunity to express their opinions at a series of meetings on 'grasping revolution' which had been convened by Zhou Enlai. Their protest, reported to Mao, who took it as a challenge to his leadership, was dismissed as the 'February adverse current.'

The army, which under Lin Biao had been ideologically trained to back Mao, was to be an essential factor in restoring order. It suited Mao's interests that it should play a political and educational role and be linked with the radicals. On 7 March he directed that the army should move into the universities, the middle schools and the higher classes of primary schools to give military and political training. On 10 March he announced that revolutionary committees comprising radical leaders of the masses, party cadres and the army should take over the administration of all institutions throughout China. Eventually this device, the three-in-one committee, was to be the new feature of Mao's

China as it emerged from the chaos, but for the moment violence and factionalism were in full spate.

Meanwhile at the Standing Committee of the Politburo in March 1967 Mao had only five supporters, Lin Biao, Zhou Enlai, Chen Boda, Kang Sheng, and Li Fuchun, against five opponents, Liu Shaoqi, Deng Xiaoping, Tao Zhu, Zhu De and Chen Yun. Mao therefore had to use his casting vote as Chairman to get a majority.

For whatever reason Mao had not finished stirring up the Red Guards. On 6 April he told them 'Have no fear of chaos. The more chaos you dish up the better. Disorder and chaos are always a good thing. They clarify things. But never use weapons.'[18] There was plenty of disorder in 1967. Many individuals were the targets of struggle sessions, notably Deng Xiaoping's son, who jumping in desperation out of a window was left paralysed from the waist down. Liu's wife was dressed in supposedly fancy clothes, high heels and a necklace of ping-pong balls, and paraded before 300,000 at Qinghua University. Liu himself disappeared.

Red Guards denounced Chen Yi, Vice-premier and Foreign Minister for his 'revisionist' foreign policy. They set fire to the office of the British Chargé d'Affaires and took Reuters correspondent, Anthony Grey, into solitary confinement for twenty-six months. For a short time they even took control of the Foreign Ministry in Beijing and sent instructions to overseas posts. China's relations with many countries were strained by extreme and irrational actions. With Burma the friendship carefully cultivated over many years ended when the Burmese government forbade children to wear Mao badges in school; riotous incidents occurred in Rangoon, and Beijing responded by calling for the overthrow of the Burmese government by the Burmese Communist Party. In London the staff at the Chinese Chargé d'Affaires office attacked the policemen on duty in Portland Place on the grounds that they were conspiring with members of the Campaign for Nuclear Disarmament who had burnt a copy of the Little Red Book as a protest against the testing of China's hydrogen bomb in June 1967.

If Mao's supporters had temporarily gone off their heads, what about the Chairman himself? In fact there is consistency in Mao's policy, if not always in his words. He was determined to put down, and indeed if necessary eliminate, his opponents, whom he saw as pursuing reactionary policies. Since late 1963 he had been teaching that the concept of 'uniting two into one' was a revisionist formula for complacency and conciliation while 'one divides into two' was the (correct) formula for continuing revolution. He had long believed that conflict was an inevitable concomitant of contradiction – an essential element in a healthy society with an ongoing revolutionary spirit.

When the revolution got out of control, he used the army to restore order, but in the three-in-one committees there was still an element of popular involvement. It followed that education was important and in 1967 Mao's educational guidelines came to the fore. These stressed practical application over mere book knowledge. Party cadres must learn from the people, they must go to the countryside and get their hands dirty. This was to be the principle of the May 7th cadre schools. A directive of 7 May 1966 was the inspiration for later sending cadres of all ranks to selected farms where they did manual work with the peasants and revived their understanding of 'serving the people' and what they owed to Mao Zedong. Theoretically it was a privilege to be chosen. Some told foreign visitors that they had applied to go and had been honoured to be selected.

The political and educational radicalism of the Cultural Revolution was in contrast to the changes in the countryside where the mass organization of the commune had been relinquished in favour of initiative at brigade and team level.[19] One important change was that the unit of accounting, i.e. the value of workpoints earned, was calculated at local level instead of at distant commune headquarters. Thus the peasants were rewarded for the achievements of their own team rather than as contributors to a large impersonal system. They were also allowed to cultivate small private plots.

The idea of developing small-scale industries in the countryside, which had gone wrong during the Great Leap Forward, was taken up again as a corollary to the modernization of agriculture. Decentralization of industry also appeared desirable in view of the military threat from the Soviet Union, notably in 1969.[20]

What of the future? Mao said that further revolutions would be necessary He invoked the analogy of a healthy body inhaling oxygen and exhaling carbon dioxide. 'A proletarian party must also get rid of the stale and take in the fresh, for only thus can it be full of vitality.[21]

THE CULTURAL REVOLUTION BECOMES INSTITUTIONALIZED

By 1968 Mao was acting to curtail blatant Red Guard excesses, which had included seizing weapons destined for Vietnam and the slaughter exemplified by the many headless corpses drifting down the Pearl River into the sea near Hong Kong. The army was given unequivocal orders to suppress disorder in the cities which they did with some enthusiasm: some eighteen million Red Guards were moved 'to the countryside,' often to remote areas. When some Red Guard leaders protested that a 'black hand' was acting against them, Mao took full responsibility saying 'I am the black hand'.

As the wilder revolutionary elements were brought under control the Cultural Revolution became institutionalized. With the clampdown maintained by the army and the military presence in the three-in-one committees, the visible manifestations of Maoism continued to prevail. As well as the Little Red Book, carried by everyone as a catechism to be quoted as well as a symbol of devotion, everyone wore a Mao badge. The green PLA fatigues favoured by the Red Guards gave way to the standard blue jacket, trousers and caps. This was the uniform of the masses to which everyone (theoretically) aspired to belong. No matter that the fine woollen suit of a top cadre was materially different from that of a manual worker, the colour was the same. Moreover, it was a unisex garment and did something to emphasize an equality of the sexes.

The new look in the arts promoted by Mao's wife Jiang Qing was dedicated to 'serving the people'; thus traditional Beijing opera was replaced by revolutionary ballet such as the Red Detachment of Women. Museums which had not been vandalized by Red Guards were reorganized to expose feudalism and justify revolution, as in the excavations at Ban Po near Xian which featured the bodies of starved children.

Big statues of Mao began to appear in public halls, parks and on university campuses. With the cult of Mao, encouraged particularly by Lin Biao and the army, went renewed emphasis on Mao's ideals of education. Now that the power struggle had resulted in the destruction of Mao's enemies, and the People's Liberation Army was in command, the revolution had indeed become cultural. The sloganizing, the paeans to the Great Helmsman became routine.

When the schools re-opened the curriculum was heavily indoctrinated with the sayings of Mao; from infant classes upwards periods were devoted to identifying with the peasants (working in the school gardens) and to productive labour (helping to process goods for local factories). A military analogy prevailed, with classes identified as companies and platoons. It was several years before schools and colleges were fully operational. Teacher training colleges spent much time preparing themselves for their new ethical role in what was then seen as the aftermath and summation of the Cultural Revolution. One important debate was about entry qualifications. Mao had railed against teachers who set traps for students. He recommended open book examinations; his supporters argued that the test for entry to higher education should be the class consciousness of the candidate and the recommendation of his unit. Well into the 1970s they fought a rearguard action against the reintroduction of exams. One fervent youth, Zhang Tiesheng, who said he had been too busy doing productive labour to find time for academic study handed in an exam paper with only his signature on it, and was cited as a hero by those opposed to entrance exams – for a time; he was later denounced as an ass.[22] In so far as Mao's reforms were challenging the old traditions of elite education for the few, rote learning, and a narrowly bookish approach, they could be seen as having a positive aspect. However, conventional wisdom in China today condemns the ten lost years of a generation deprived of proper education. Similarly those who were sent to the countryside or 'volunteered' for May 7th cadre schools almost invariably look back in anger at the way they were treated.[23]

With the restoration of order former cadres reappeared. The Party began to take the leading role in the revolutionary committees, and the State Planning Commission, with some of its old personnel, was restored.

Liu Shaoqi was officially removed from his post as head of state in October 1968. It was later disclosed that, seriously ill after harsh treatment, he died in squalor on 12 November 1969. Lin Biao was confirmed as Mao's successor at the Ninth Congress of the Party, which met on 1 April 1969. Soldiers comprised 40 per cent of the new Central Committee, and of the Politburo of sixteen, ten were military men, but only three were clear supporters of Lin Biao. If the balance of power still resided in the army and Lin Biao, we now know that at that very time Mao was beginning to have doubts about Lin's suitability for the succession.

THE PROBLEM OF LIN BIAO

Since Liu Shaoqi's downfall, the post of head of state had been in abeyance. At a Central Committee Plenum in August 1970, when the draft for a new state constitution was being discussed, Lin proposed that the post be revived. He also proposed Mao for Head of State no doubt hoping to succeed to the position himself. Mao saw to it that this proposal was squashed. Moreover, Lin Biao with Chen Boda also proposed that the Party should recognize the special genius of Mao Zedong. Mao objected to this presumably because he saw it as a ploy to enhance their own role. Chen Boda, as Lin Biao's ally, was out of favour with Mao and was demoted.[24]

Lin did not have to be paranoid to consider himself under threat. During 1971 Lin's supporters in the military came under attack in a policy which was later described by Mao as 'throwing stones, adding sand to mud, and undermining the cornerstone'.[25] The 'stones' aimed at Lin's lieutenants were demands that they make self-criticisms of their behaviour during the August 1970 plenum, the 'sand' was the replacement of some of Lin's supporters in the Military Affairs commission of the CCP Central Committee and the 'cornerstone' was the military force around Beijing where some of the leaders were also replaced.

Lin Biao was on the way out. Did he in desperation plan to assassinate Mao? According to the official story his son masterminded a plan – Project 571 (This number is a pun in Chinese meaning armed uprising) which involved intercepting and attacking Mao's train with dynamite, bazookas and artillery. At the time of the alleged attack in August 1971 Mao was certainly on a train touring south and central China. The story goes that the attack was made on the wrong train or coach, Mao returned unscathed to Beijing and Lin Biao and his fellow conspirators, realizing the game was up, took over a military passenger plane (a British-built Trident) at a naval airbase near Beidaihe resort and ordered the pilot to fly to Moscow. The plane which did not have enough fuel crashed just over the border in the Mongolian People's Republic.

There are several problems with this story. Would such a skilled politician and top military strategist as Lin Biao have thought of such a hare-brained assassination scheme or allowed it to go forward under the command of his 27 year old son?[26] A plane did crash in Mongolia after bursting into flames; there were no survivors and it was not clear that the human remains included proof of Lin's presence. Recently released evidence now suggests that he was there but it is still possible that his dead body was put on the plane.

In an alternative scenario Lin was not on the plane: those who took flight did so after their leader Lin had been assassinated after a last dinner party with Mao and Zhou at a villa in the Western Hills. They had a feast with some rare delicacies, drank a rare old imperial wine and talked of old times. After an emotional farewell they watched their guest depart. As his car reached the bottom of the driveway it was blown to smithereens by mortar fire.[27]

There was no announcement at the time. The annual 1 October celebrations for national day did not take place in 1971: presumably to avoid having to explain Lin's absence from the reviewing stand. Only later was the official story of Lin's attempted flight released.

ASSESSING THE CULTURAL REVOLUTION

In Mao's view the Cultural Revolution was over by the turn of the decade. Therefore it seems that he was defining it as the period of struggle against his enemies, the revisionists, which was indeed a time of violent revolution. The alternative view that the Cultural Revolution covered the whole ten years from 1966 to 1976 defines it not simply as political upheaval but as a period of Maoist indoctrination and dominance.

Although the disorderly disruption was over, Mao's political programme was still being implemented and his guidelines were not seriously challenged while he lived.

What had been achieved and what were the consequences by 1970?

1 Mao had apparently overcome the revisionists but he had not solved the problem of revisionism in a socialist party. His opponents, notably Deng Xiaoping, were soon back on the 'capitalist road'.

2 For many of Mao's supporters idealism was to give way to disillusion. However, some Red Guards have said that being radicalized in the Cultural Revolution had prepared them for later dissent in the 1980s. They had had experience of criticizing their elders.

3 The main losers were the intellectuals. In comparing the Cultural Revolution with the Great Leap Forward it is notable that the latter being largely economic, the masses had suffered most, whereas in the Cultural Revolution, which was essentially political, it was the elite who suffered most. The peasants had benefited by the changes made in the aftermath of the Great Leap, and agricultural production was not much affected by Cultural Revolution politics.

4 As for the number of victims, it has been estimated that approximately 500,000 died during the Cultural Revolution.[28] In addition, many who survived endured the trauma of torture and abuse. Their sufferings have been well documented in numerous accounts. Few, if any, are now prepared to say that they benefited from rustication.

5 Perhaps the most far-reaching consequence was that higher education in particular had been interrupted and was not fully restored until well into the 1970s. It is said that a generation lost its schooling. Even if this is an exaggeration, there is no doubt that the country suffered from a shortage of trained personnel for a

decade. Many young people were personally deprived and China's economy was accordingly handicapped at the very time when the opening to the outside world offered the possibility of new development. While Mao was alive there was a question mark over the role of intellectuals and the part they could play in modernization.

EXPLANATIONS

Official Chinese explanations put the blame for the chaotic excesses of the Cultural Revolution on Maoist extremists, and in convenient retrospect on the Gang of Four in particular. Mao rightly looms large since the Cultural Revolution was at least in part a leadership struggle, and he played a key role in promoting the chain of events. But it is necessary to consider the wider social factors which contributed to such a major social and political upheaval.

What was the pent-up force unleashed by Mao and how in Chinese society had it originated? Were participants merely echoing Mao's slogans or were they revolutionaries inspired with their own agenda, such as ideas of egalitarianism or the perceived interests of their own class label?

The Cultural Revolution must be seen as a culmination of past practices. From its beginning the CCP had, as a means of enforcing compliance, directed mass campaigns. The process of public denunciation and struggle sessions involving violence had featured in land reform and in the three-Anti and five -Anti campaigns and in the anti-rightist backlash to the 100 Flowers.

Did the popular power struggle include an idealistic movement by the masses against corrupt leaders with elitist and capitalist leanings and against bureaucracy? After all, that was what it claimed to be (albeit in Maoist rhetoric). Some Western writers, discounting the adulation of Mao, have seen it in this light.[29] In contrast Klaus Mehnert says the Red Guards were created by Mao and the Cultural Revolution was a 'revolution from above'.[30]

Accepting that the Cultural Revolution was to some extent a popular movement, how far were factional struggles based on class interests? The labelling of social classes and political elements had not only affected the careers of individuals, it had also created groups with common interests.[31] We have noted the opposing factions of Red Guards. Those from cadres' families wanted to preserve their status; by purging corruption they would preserve the Party. Those labelled with bourgeois origin, having lain low since the campaigns of the 1950s now seized the chance to rise up and form rival Red Guard groups.[32] They had the incentive to correct years of injustice against their families. In a fluid situation local leaders fought to maintain or extend their privileges. Such were the pent-up forces, explosive enough to explain the furious years of the Cultural Revolution.

7 A Great Power triangle, 1964–79

Foreign affairs did not play a major role in the Cultural Revolution. Conversely the effect of the Cultural Revolution on foreign relations tended to be negative, its ideological line reinforcing China's isolation. In 1964 China was indeed isolated. The rift with the Soviet Union was publicly acknowledged. The People's Republic remained excluded from the United Nations and subject to boycott by the United States while US military involvement in Vietnam was escalating. China appeared liable to attack on two fronts. As the Cultural Revolution came under control in 1968–9 the leadership embarked on a new foreign policy initiative which reflected the national interests of China rather than ideology. By welcoming President Nixon in 1972 China made a significant move back into the community of nations.

CHINA'S ISOLATION IN THE MID-1960S AND THE PROBLEM OF VIETNAM

The fall of Nikita Khrushchev in October 1964 momentarily offered the prospect of Sino-Soviet reconciliation. When Zhou Enlai led a delegation to Moscow for the anniversary of the 1917 Bolshevik Revolution, 7 November 1964, the Soviets raised the question of increasing aid to China (as well as North Korea and Vietnam) and in return the Chinese were expected to co-operate at least to the extent of ceasing public polemics. The Chinese were not impressed by this overture. A *Red Flag* article 'Why Khrushchev Fell' on 21 November reviewed Khrushchev's incompetence and wrongheadedness in the case of *inter alia* India, Cuba and Yugoslavia, lamented his woeful departure from Marxism–Leninism, and upbraided his supporters 'the US imperialists, the reactionaries and the modern imperialists'.[1] When a preparatory committee of twenty-six government parties met in Moscow in March

1965 to plan for a full assembly of the communist parties, the Chinese refused to attend and described the meeting as a 'gloomy and forlorn affair.'

It is notable that the question of supporting Vietnam became another bone of contention between the two communist powers. The Tonkin Gulf incident (Bac Bo Gulf), when North Vietnamese torpedo boats were alleged to have attacked an American warship, was a turning point for the American involvement in Vietnam.[2] At the time of the incident, August 1964, the Soviets supported an American proposal, turned down by North Vietnam, that the matter should be referred to the UN Security Council. This prompted the Chinese to accuse Khrushchev of having 'cudgelled his brains for ways to help the US provocateurs get out of their predicament and to whitewash the criminal aggression of the US pirates'. Nor did China respond favourably when the new Soviet leadership published a strong pledge of support for North Vietnam and invited the National Liberation Front of South Vietnam to establish a permanent mission in Moscow. In April 1965 a Soviet proposal for a meeting with North Vietnamese and Chinese leaders to discuss co-operation was accepted by Hanoi and rejected by Beijing. Arrangements for the transport of Soviet supplies to North Vietnam via China led to bickering in which both sides accused the other of failing to support the struggle of the Vietnamese people.

Moreover, it is questionable whether either China or the USSR had a good reason for being engaged militarily in south-east Asia except in response to the American intervention. American aggression in Indochina was a major consideration in Lin Biao's article of 2 September 1965 ' Long Live the Victory of People's War'. From the title and tone of this statement, which cited the relevance of the Chinese rural based, revolutionary strategic model to the oppressed peoples of Asia, Africa and Latin America, it might have been supposed that China would give military support to oppressed peoples. On the contrary it could be read as a reminder to the people of Vietnam that just as the Chinese people had succeeded by themselves, so could the Vietnamese. Secret messages from Beijing to Washington stressed that China was *not* intending to commit its forces in Vietnam. In 1965 Mao had asked the Pakistani President Ayub Khan to tell Washington that the Korean war and the Vietnam war were different and to note how restrained the Chinese had been over Taiwan.[3] As for the Soviets, at this time they were mindful of their interests in reaching a *modus vivendi* with the United States in Europe and elsewhere.

Thus China and the USSR had a common interest in preferring not to be directly engaged in Vietnam. Both countries believed that limited involvement was essential to maintain a balance of power against American aggression in Asia. Such was the underlying reality of the anti-imperialist slogans at the time.

THE MOUNTING THREAT FROM THE USSR: CHINA'S ROLE IN A GREAT POWER TRIANGLE

As a result of the Sino-Soviet Rift the previous division of the world into two blocs was transformed into a great power triangle. If China was less than a full superpower, it was nevertheless an independent and significant force. Among those who recognized the importance of China's diplomatic position was Richard Nixon, who in an article published in *Foreign Affairs* in October 1967 entitled significantly 'Asia after Vietnam', wrote 'Any American policy towards Asia must come urgently to grips with the reality of China . . . Taking the long view, we simply can not afford to leave China forever outside the family of nations, there to mature its fantasies, cherish its hates and threaten its neighbours.'

In spite of the brouhaha of Red Guardism and the Chinese polemics on revolution in the Third World, it is not easy to see how China was threatening its neighbours at that time. On the contrary, China itself had grounds for feeling threatened. On its southern border the United States was deploying massive force on behalf of the puppet regime in South Vietnam. On the northern border were nearly forty Soviet divisions, some recently moved from Eastern Europe.[4] As early as 1965 Mao had told the Pakistani President Ayub Khan that the USA and the USSR were seeking an understanding which would lead to the containment of China. Indeed in October 1966 President Johnson sought agreement with the Soviets on European issues in order to 'achieve reconciliation'. There is evidence that the Soviets in summer 1969 discussed a contingency plan for destroying China's nuclear capability.

Confrontational incidents on the long border between China and the Soviet Union had increased annually. In March 1969 military confrontation erupted into fighting over a disputed island in the Ussuri River. Zhen Bao (Precious Treasure) island is frequently flooded and normally uninhabited. The Chinese attacked first. Why? The Soviet Union had been strengthening its border forces especially to the east of Lake Baikal. It was militarily appropriate to strike first and make the Soviets aware of the limits to their high-handed action as well as to make the political point that the Chinese people were threatened by the Soviet revisionists. The incident would draw attention away from internal problems and momentarily enhance the authority of Lin Biao, the Minister of Defence.

The military scuffle was largely a media matter in which both sides blamed the other and it soon passed.[5] More serious for the Chinese was Moscow's policy of containment which in 1969 could be seen in visits by Alexei Kosygin and Soviet diplomats to India, Pakistan, Afghanistan, North Korea, Mongolia, Burma, Laos, Cambodia and Japan. Kosygin proposed a regional economic group of India, Pakistan, Iran, Afghanistan and the Soviet Union. Leonid Brezhnev, General Secretary of the Soviet Communist Party, while continuing to cite imperialism as a major obstacle, also attacked Maoism and 'those people who would like to bind the chains of a new slavery around the young national states'. By December 1969 Moscow was openly discussing a collective security plan for Asia.

After the Ussuri confrontation Moscow made proposals for talks which were ignored by Beijing. Meanwhile the Soviets increased their forces on the Soviet border, a *Pravda* article indicated that any Sino–Soviet conflict would inevitably be nuclear and the United States and other countries were asked how they would react in the event of a Soviet attack on China. If all this was designed to induce the Chinese to come to the conference table, it worked. On 11 September 1969 Kosygin and Zhou Enlai met at Beijing airport. Eventually Kosygin's proposal for talks on the border was accepted on 7 October. It was agreed that even if there was no settlement of the disputed borders, the status quo should be maintained and there should be no use of force. This in itself was indicative of a new phase in Sino-Soviet relations. It also reflected the fact that the Cultural Revolution had calmed down.

SINO-AMERICAN RAPPROCHMENT

The main factors leading to diplomatic détente between China and the United States were:

1 The increase in the Soviet forces, both conventional and nuclear which were seen to constitute a threat to the security of China.
2 The difficult position of the United States in Vietnam. Attempts to get out began with President Johnson and became a keystone of incoming President Nixon's policy.
3 The prospect of US–Soviet collusion, exemplified by the US, USSR, UK Partial Test Ban Treaty in 1963, and further advanced

in 1967 at a meeting between President Johnson and Alexei Kosygin in June which led to a draft nuclear non-proliferation treaty in August. Moves towards US–Soviet rapprochment came to a head in January 1969 when Nixon in his inaugural address announced his intention to co-operate further with the Soviet Union.

4   If the Americans were in an impasse over Vietnam, the Chinese were equally stymied over Taiwan. Détente with the US might lead the US to be less intransigent in its support for the nationalist regime on the island.

5   There could have been an economic rationale for détente with the USA, since it would lead to the opening-up of trade, particularly to China's advantage. But this reason does not appear in the Chinese materials sent out to party members in December 1971 to justify détente.[6]

Ancillary factors were the enthusiasm of the key players on both sides. Chairman Mao was happy as the prospect unfolded of China emerging from isolation to be recognized as a world power. Nixon relished the idea of winning a second term in office by an apparently daring and imaginative coup. Why did it take more than two years to set up the Nixon visit to Beijing?

CHINESE POLITICS

Is there a clear relationship between the political factionalizing inside China and foreign policy? We have noted in Chapter 6 that from the time around April 1969, when Lin Biao was confirmed as Mao's successor, Mao had doubts about his suitability. Thereafter the leadership can be defined in three main groups: the radicals with Jiang Qing and other enthusiasts of the Cultural Revolution; the military, Lin Biao and other army and navy leaders and the moderates headed by Premier Zhou Enlai. How was foreign policy affected by the interplay of these factions in the lead up to the Nixon visit?

The Chinese proposed on 26 November 1968 that the Warsaw ambassadorial talks should be reconvened in February 1969. Zhou Enlai was behind this initiative, which was timed to coincide with the coming to office of President Nixon. However, opponents in the Chinese leadership successfully opposed and forced the cancellation of the planned Sino-American meeting in Warsaw. It has been accepted by some writers[7] that Zhou Enlai favoured détente and was opposed by

Lin Biao. The evidence for this is little more than a casual remark made by Mao to Richard Nixon that a group opposing the policy of détente 'got on an airplane and fled abroad'. Lin fitted; he had fled and was dead. Another comment by Zhou Enlai in December 1971 was that Lin had made accusations that the people of Vietnam had been betrayed.[8] Apart from these two remarks any assertion that Lin Biao opposed Mao and Zhou Enlai on the question of détente with America depends on speculating from his political circumstances: (1) as Minister of Defence Lin favoured confrontation leading to increased military expenditure; (2) Lin was a main force behind a pro-Soviet tilt in 1970; (3) a diplomatic success by Zhou Enlai would strengthen his position against Lin in any competition for the succession; (4) it is assumed that Lin was opposed because the decline in Lin's power closely coincided with the rapprochement.

The theory does not stand up well to further examination: (1) the fact that defence expenditure was sustained during this period is attributable to Mao rather than Lin; (2) Both moderates and the military faction agreed to the 1970 'tilt' towards the USSR. The military faction was still strong in early 1970 and internal politics decreed that the moderates would do well to cooperate with them to rebuild the Party and suppress the Cultural Revolution; (3) Zhou Enlai had good reason for feeling rebuffed by the United States. At a press conference on 27 January 1970 Nixon announced that although he looked forward to reopening the Warsaw ambassadorial meetings, if they were to succeed the Chinese must first change their position. At the same conference he announced new negotiations with the Soviet Union to limit strategic nuclear arms. It is not surprising that the Warsaw talks, due to begin on 20 February were cancelled on the 19th. On 30 April US and South Vietnamese forces invaded Cambodia, an affront to China's long-held policy of safe-guarding Cambodian independence. To the military faction this was evidence of the Americans' aggressive intentions. In all the circumstances the tilt can be interpreted as a generally agreed policy of keeping options open and playing hard to get with the Americans.

In general Zhou took care to avoid antagonizing Lin and if Lin had doubts about the new foreign policy initiatives he kept them to himself. It has been suggested that Lin's interest in foreign affairs was confined to the military perspective and that he did not intrude into the diplomatic area dominated by Zhou and Mao. The memoirs of Lin's secretary Zhang Yunsheng indicate that his master had so little interest in foreign policy that he fell asleep during a briefing on Cambodia in May 1970.[9]

THE AMERICAN APPROACH TO CHINA

Soon after coming to power Nixon explored the possibility of negotiation with China to strengthen his hand against the Soviet Union and to find a way out of the Vietnam War. In addition to suggesting that the ambassadorial talks be resumed, the US also opened a secret line of communication via President Yahya Kahn of Pakistan. Of the non-Communist countries Pakistan had particularly close relations with Beijing and had played an important part in easing relations between China and Canada, Iran and Turkey.

Nixon explains that during 1969 the Chinese ignored the 'few low-level signals of interest we sent them.' Nixon took what he described as 'the first serious public step in the China initiative in February 1970' when he sent a foreign policy report to Congress declaring that it was in the US interest to take 'what steps we can toward improved practical relations with Peking.'[10] Then in March American restrictions on travel to China were lifted and in April trade controls began to be reduced. Throughout 1970 signals continued to be exchanged via the presidents of Pakistan and Romania. On 9 December Zhou sent a message via Yahya Khan that Nixon's representative would be welcome in Beijing to discuss the question of Taiwan. Zhou stressed that the message did not come from him alone; it had also been approved by Chairman Mao and Lin Biao. The Americans replied via the Pakistani ambassador that any discussions should not be limited to Taiwan and suggested exploring the possibility of a high-level meeting in Beijing.

By the end of 1970 the messages were coming thick and fast and were unambiguous.[11] As Zhou Enlai summed up: Nixon wanted to come and we were willing to talk with him, because if you do not talk with the head who else should you talk with? This of course is an over-simplification for the period 1968–71. Zhou had done much more than react to the American proposals.

Throughout the first half of 1971 both the Chinese and American peoples were kept in ignorance. When in February the United States instigated the invasion of Laos by the South Vietnamese, the *People's Daily* trumpeted 'Don't Lose Your Head, Nixon'. Then on 6 April came a totally unexpected invitation for an American table tennis team in Japan to go on to play several exhibition matches in China. When Vice-President Agnew at a press conference told reporters that the media coverage of the table tennis visit was an undesirable propaganda triumph for China, Nixon had to tell him to keep off the topic. On 27 April another message from Zhou Enlai came via Yahya Khan stressing that, while Taiwan remained the main problem, the Chinese were now ready to have direct discussions and reaffirmed their 'willingness to receive publicly in Peking a special envoy of the President of the U.S. for instance, Mr Kissinger or the U.S. Secretary of State or even the President of the U.S. himself for a direct meeting and discussion.' As Nixon said, this raised as many problems as it solved. It was clear that the matter must be kept secret lest conservative opposition in Congress should 'scuttle the entire effort'.

HENRY KISSINGER'S VISIT

Pending a formal reply Henry Kissinger told Yahya Khan to tell Zhou Enlai that communications should be confined to the Pakistani channel 'until an official link was securely in place.' The White House was worried that China might approach other leading Americans. Indeed Beijing had three prospective Democratic candidates in mind – Senators Kennedy, McGovern and Muskie. The tip-off had come from an American reporter who had been quizzed on alternative invitations during the table tennis visit. Kissinger's warning forestalled the invitations to the Democrats.

The question remained: who should go to China to set up Nixon's visit? Consideration ranged over many candidates from David Bruce to George Bush. One man not on the list was the Secretary of State, William Rogers. He was kept in the dark. Ignorant, he made a public statement that any rapprochment with China might eventually be possible provided that China showed her willingness to comply with 'the rules of international law'.[12] When Nixon, to counter the possible damage of this statement, referred to a possible visit to China 'sometime in some capacity' and mentioned various options for solving the Taiwan impasse, the Chinese strongly denounced any suggestion that Taiwan's status was unsettled. This was a clear warning against shilly-shallying which was understood by Kissinger. He prepared himself for the role of envoy by reading a bag of books on China. Then with the connivance of Joseph Farland, American ambassador in Pakistan, a 'completely covert' visit of 48 hours was arranged. Within this 'unbreakable deadline' Kissinger and Zhou Enlai engineered the groundwork for a presidential visit. In retrospect Kissinger dwelt on crossing the Rubicon and the penalty of failure – 'continued isolation for one side and sharpened international difficulties for the other.'[13] It would give heart to the Soviets, turn retreat in Indochina into a rout and of course make an ass of Nixon in America.

Henry Kissinger following a public visit to Pakistan disappeared. Worldly-wise reporters assumed his secret rendezvous was with a girl-friend on a houseboat in Kashmir. In fact he had flown secretly to Beijing for the period from 9 to 11 July.[14] Nixon later joked that Henry's reputation since his divorce had been an ingredient of the plot. The secret was kept until, on 15 July, Nixon astounded the world, as well as his close colleagues, by announcing that he had accepted an invitation to visit China.

One of the early effects of this statement was on the question of the China seat at the United Nations. In late October countries which for years had been obeying the American command to vote against the People's Republic changed their mind and voted for an Albanian motion to seat the Communists.[15] As they walked in, the Nationalists walked out; for them, too, there could be only 'one sun in the heaven'. If events at the UN moved faster than Washington had intended, the USA made no bones about accepting the outcome. In the event it was part of the stage set for Nixon's triumphal visit to Beijing in February 1972.

THE NIXON VISIT

Given the months of anticipation between the Kissinger visit and the Nixon visit the joint communiqué issued in Shanghai on 27 February 1972 might well have been considered an anti-climax. The fact that it was not is a consequence both of the way it was stage-managed and the fact that both sides genuinely welcomed the opening-up 'of new prospects for the relations between the two countries'.

The biggest stumbling block was not of course the Indochina war, both sides wanted to see the end of that, but Taiwan. The US had been committed to the military defence of the nationalist government on Taiwan since 1954. Beijing had always vehemently asserted Taiwan's status as a province of the motherland. Most important for the Chinese was the American assertion that the US did 'not challenge that position', believed in a peaceful settlement of the Taiwan issue by the Chinese themselves and affirmed 'the ultimate objective of the withdrawal of all US forces and military installations from Taiwan'. So the communiqué was a statement of differences which should be settled short of war and agreement in principle to extend diplomatic and cultural contacts leading to 'normalization'.[16]

To what extent had Nixon's visit been a victory for the Chinese? The Chinese leadership certainly thought it was. In an internal report to the

Party in December 1971 Zhou Enlai explained why it had been right to accede to Nixon's request for a visit. It was cited as a victory for the people of the world, to which the internal pressure of the US people had contributed resulting in rendering 'bankrupt the China policy of the US'. The expansion of Soviet interests in Europe and the Middle East consequent on the Americans being bogged down in Vietnam had given the Americans no choice but to improve relations with China. Therefore it was 'necessary to take full advantage of the contradiction between the US and the USSR and magnify it'. Nixon had asked to come and would have to bring 'something in his pocket'. It was he who would have some explaining to do at home if the negotiation failed.[17]

WHAT WERE THE IMMEDIATE RESULTS?

The Chinese had put the broader issues of China's security before any immediate settlement of the Taiwan question. As Mao said to Kissinger in November 1973, 'I say we can do without Taiwan for the time being . . . Do not take matters on this world so rapidly'.[18]

With the prospect of 'normalization' in their relations with the US, the Chinese no longer felt threatened by the prospect of war on two fronts and were less likely to be pressured by anti-Chinese collusion between the US and the USSR. While the Chinese tacitly accepted the US military presence in the Western Pacific, the Shanghai Communiqué did not specifically mention the US–Japanese Mutual Security Pact.[19] Instead it noted Chinese opposition to the 'revival and outward expansion of Japanese militarism' and support for an 'independent, democratic, peaceful, and neutral Japan.'

The Japanese had been discussing the prospects for improving relations with China for several years. In April 1970 some Japanese firms accepted the four principles of trade which had been laid down by Beijing. Companies trading with China: (1) must not trade with Taiwan or South Korea; (2) must not invest in Taiwan or South Korea; (3) must not export weapons for US use in Indochina; (4) must not affiliate with American firms in Japan in joint ventures or subsidiaries in China. The shock news of the Nixon visit helped to speed up the process of improving relations, particularly after the Tanaka government was installed on 7 July 1972. Again the status of Taiwan was the paramount consideration. The Chinese insisted on three principles: (1) recognition of the PRC as the sole legal government of China; (2) that Taiwan was an inalienable part of Chinese territory; (3) the abrogation of the treaty between Japan and Taiwan. When Tanaka indicated acceptance, he was invited to visit Beijing in the wake of cultural exchanges including the Japanese volleyball team. On 29 September 1972 a joint statement heralded a new era in Sino-Japanese relations.

China's international status had risen considerably thanks to the publicity of Nixon's visit. During 1972 nineteen nations in addition to Japan hastened to establish or restore relations with Beijing.

There was no concomitant warming in Sino-Soviet relations. The Soviet–Indian Friendship Treaty in August 1971 and Soviet support for India in the Bangladesh war were cited as evidence that the Soviet Union intended to use India to extend its 'aggressive' influence in Asia.

Moreover, the Chinese suspected with reason that the long-term US policy was to improve relations with the Soviet Union. After all, Nixon had visited Moscow less than three months after his China visit to sign the SALT agreement in May 1972. This meeting produced a goodwill document stating the principles of relations between the superpowers.

The triumphant re-election of President Nixon in November 1972 and the Paris Peace Accords signed between the United States and North Vietnam in January 1973 might have led the Chinese to expect that further development of the détente would follow. When Kissinger visited Beijing in February 1973, Mao told him that Sino-American trade was 'pitiful' and that 'China would have to go to school abroad' implying that both American trade and expertise would be welcome. After twenty-three years the Chinese leader was again expressing his willingness to do business.[20]

In 1973 liaison offices were opened in Beijing and Washington. Thereafter the development of the new relationship made little progress between 1973 and 1976. It was not helped by the crises in succession to the leadership which affected both China and the United States. In Washington, undermined by the Watergate accusations, Nixon became increasingly dependent on the right-wing of the Republican Party which was traditionally committed to upholding the Taiwan regime. The American election of 1976 produced a Democratic president, Jimmy Carter, who while pursuing a second SALT agreement with the USSR was not anxious to give priority to speeding up 'normalization' with China. In mid-1977 a Gallup poll indicated that giving up Taiwan would not be a popular course of action. The administration hinted that so far as China was concerned Carter would do whatever was necessary in his second administration. Deng Xiao-ping, worried by the actions of the Soviet 'hegemonists' who had seized power in Afghanistan and extended Soviet influence in the horn of Africa, was willing to promise that China would not use force to take Taiwan. Nor would he object if the USA continued to sell arms to Taiwan. From the autumn of 1978 the Carter administration moved towards a settlement, encouraged by American businessmen attracted as ever by the legendary China market. When Deng flew to America in February 1978, he reiterated the Chinese position for a peaceful settlement of the Taiwan problem. The Americans were also reassured by the CIA's assessment that the island could defend itself against Beijing's inadequate amphibious forces. Normalization was nigh. During a highly publicized visit to the United States Deng was feted; on 1 March China received the accolade of full diplomatic recognition by the United States. The ultimate price was the withdrawal of American recognition from the Republic of China on Taiwan.

'TEACHING VIETNAM A LESSON'

The lustre reflected on Deng by this diplomatic achievement was to be tarnished by China's quarrel with Vietnam.

Relations between the PRC and Vietnam had been deteriorating. Chinese residents in Vietnam had been fleeing both by sea and by land to escape discriminatory treatment. Soviet links to Vietnam were confirmed in a friendship treaty in October 1978 which allowed the USSR to use naval facilities in Vietnam. Then in December 1978 Vietnam invaded Kampuchea to remove Pol Pot and his extremely vicious Khmer Rouge government which was supported by China. In February 80,000 Chinese troops attacked along the Vietnamese border. They intended to inflict a short sharp defeat as in the Sino-Indian War of 1962. But this time they were less successful. At the cost of great casualties they captured frontier positions and provincial towns but they withdrew leaving Vietnam still in Kampuchea. The Chinese withdrawal began on 5 March and was completed on 16 March.

Deng Xiaoping claimed to have taught Vietnam a lesson. In fact the lesson learned was quite different. It was that China could no longer mount a successful military attack even against a war-weary weak neighbour like Vietnam. China's forces needed modernization. Although the invasion was militarily rather a disaster, it had a diplomatic pay-off. China had demonstrated that it was positively anti-Soviet, a ploy in the triangular relationship which encouraged the United States to initiate military cooperation and to see China as a partner whose economic well-being should be advanced.

8 A decade of transition, 1972–81

While Mao was alive there could be no fundamental change. The opposition of the Gang of Four and other radical diehards which led to the abrupt dismissal of Deng in April 1976 forestalled plans for modernization. But extreme Maoist convictions were likely to lead to economic stagnation since they discouraged the international cooperation on which technological change increasingly depends. The death of Mao and the weakening of ideology allowed more pragmatic policies to prevail. Deng Xiaoping was re-elevated; he coaxed China onto a new road.

MAO'S LAST YEARS

At the time of President Nixon's visit in February 1972 Mao's prestige was as high as ever, but he was visibly ageing and the question of the succession, and the nature of China's ongoing socialism, had still to be resolved. With the ousting of Chen Boda and the death of Lin Biao the radicals had lost ground. Only two of the five men appointed to the Standing Committee (of the Politburo) in April 1969 remained[1], Mao and Zhou Enlai. Zhou had masterminded the Nixon visit and continued to administer the country as premier. However, from the summer of 1972 he knew he had cancer and from May 1973 he spent much time in hospital, although he continued to make public appearances with a brave face which belied his deteriorating condition.

The leading radicals, who wished to continue Cultural Revolution policies, were Mao's wife Jiang Qing and two of her associates Zhang Chunqiao and Yao Wenyuan. In August 1973 at the Tenth Party Congress they were promoted to the Politburo and Zhang Chunqiao was appointed to the Standing Committee. Also promoted was a protégé of Jiang Qing, Wang Hongwen, formerly a cotton mill worker and

Cultural Revolution activist, who became second vice-chairman of the Party. These four were the Shanghai group later to be vilified as the Gang of Four.

The 'moderates' led by Zhou Enlai quietly pressed ahead with economic development. By 1969 industrial output was already recovering from the poor showing in 1967–8. Now in the context of a Five-Year Plan, 1971–5, fresh policies gave scope to material incentives and to central planning, in contrast to the Maoist emphasis on moral incentives and decentralization. Industrial production (light and heavy) generally improved until 1974 when it dropped almost to zero and then picked up again in 1975.[2] The figures for grain production to 1975 also show growth, except for a year of bad weather in 1972, rising to per capita levels of 1956–7.

The strength of the radicals was in their hold over propaganda. After the Tenth Congress the campaign to 'Criticize Confucius' was started. This involved a pun: the Confucian *Analects* were quoted to criticize the actions of the twelfth century statesman, the Duke of Zhou, and the target was Zhou Enlai's programmes. Then at the instigation of the moderates the campaign was extended by adding Lin Biao's name. By summer 1974 the movement to criticize Lin Biao and Confucius was restrained by order of the Politburo which also ordered attention to be shifted from 'grasping revolution' to promoting production. Among those rehabilitated and elected to the Central Committee at the Tenth Congress was Deng Xiaoping. By the time of the Fourth National People's Congress in January 1975 he had risen to vice-premier, chairing the State Council in Premier Zhou's absence. He was also vice-chairman of the Party with a seat on the standing committee of the Politburo and he was head (chief of staff) of the armed forces. The congress gave formal approval to a programme for modernizing 'agriculture, industry, national defence and science and technology' which came to be known as the 'Four Modernizations'.

In pursuing the new policies Deng was associated with the ailing Zhou, but Mao was ambivalent in his support for Deng. While backing Deng's programme he also put forward leftist views critical of the pragmatic approach which, for example, increased wage differentials. He also encouraged Zhang Chunqiao and Yao Wenyuan to publish their views on the importance of class struggle. It has been suggested that the re-elevation of Deng was intended to 'hoodwink the military' and play for time while Mao sorted out the problem of the succession.[3] For the radicals, the rise of Deng had at least had the advantage of balancing the military.

On Zhou's death (8 January 1976) Mao felt he had to take action which would prevent Deng from becoming all-powerful and completely undoing the Cultural Revolution. He gave his blessing to Hua Guofeng, a relatively obscure official from Hunan who had risen to be Minister of Public Security. When Hua was appointed acting premier of the State Council on 3 February, replacing Zhou Enlai, there was general surprise. Mao is said to have explained the appointment as follows: 'Firstly he has had experience in work at the prefectural and provincial levels, and his performance as Minister of Public Security over the past several years is not bad. Secondly, he is loyal and honest. Thirdly he is not stupid.'[4] It is not clear whether Mao was consciously appointing his successor. Presumably he hoped that Hua with his solid, unsparkling credentials could be seen as a compromise choice acceptable for the time being to the radicals on the left and the moderates on the right.

However, Hua's appointment as 'acting Premier'[5] annoyed the radicals, particularly Zhang Chunqiao, who had hoped to become Premier. The radicals tried to play down the mourning for Zhou by not announcing where the cremation ceremony would take place and they tried to hush up pro-Zhou and anti-radical student demonstrations in Nanjing. This was the prelude to the popular demonstrations which occurred in Tiananmen Square at the beginning of April. The Qingming festival, the traditional time for visiting the graves of one's ancestors, modified by the Communists into an occasion for honouring the martyrs of the revolution, inspired crowds of people to converge on the square with wreaths in honour of Zhou Enlai. Mixed in with these tributes were hostile allusions to Jiang Qing and the Shanghai radicals.

> You must be mad
> To want to be an empress!
> Here's a mirror to look at yourself
> And see what you really are.
> You've got together a little gang
> To stir up trouble all the time,
> Hoodwinking the people, capering about.
> But your days are numbered ...

Mao himself was attacked under the pseudonym of the despotic emperor of Qin.

> China is no longer the China of yore,
> And the people are no longer wrapped in sheer ignorance,
> Gone for good is Qin Huang's feudal society.

When the authorities intervened, the demonstration became violent and first the police and then the militia were sent to clear the square and arrest demonstrators. The blame for this incident was put on Deng Xiaoping, who was removed from all his posts. In fact he left Beijing under military protection and subsequently had meetings with several army leaders to discuss the future. Momentarily Jiang Qing's influence seemed to rise. Her power depended, however, not only on Maoist tradition, but on Mao himself, and in the summer of 1976 the old man was fading fast. It happened that there occurred severe drought and earthquakes, culminating in July with the worst earthquake for centuries at Tangshan. Such disasters were recognized by superstitious Chinese as the portent for the end of a dynasty. On 9 September Mao died.

HUA GUOFENG AS PARTY CHAIRMAN

How did Hua become Party Chairman when Mao died and survive at the head of the political system until 1981? He presided during a period of fundamental change but his place in history has been overshadowed, as his power was undermined, by the rise of Deng Xiaoping. If Hua's career as chairman is described as one of slow failure, at least he can be credited with holding the ring during the transitional period when ideology gave way to a new era of pragmatic reforms.

Hua's claim to legitimacy was based on some remarks Mao was alleged to have made at a meeting with Hua at the end of April after the Tiananmen Memorial incident. '1. Carry out the work slowly, not in haste; 2. Act according to past principles; 3. With you in charge I am at ease.' Then in June 1976 at the last recorded meeting with Party leaders including Hua, Mao said, 'It is my idea that there should be no presidency for the country. The best solution is for the Politburo to produce a tripartite leadership of old, middle-aged and young cadres. It is up to the Politburo to decide whether Jiang Qing shall be included.'

Matters were not so comfortably resolved. The massive earthquake at Tangshan was an occasion for Hua to show effective leadership and incidentally for the PLA to restore its image, which had been tarnished by the shooting of Red Guards and its association with the traitor Lin Biao. Mao's death soon afterwards on 9 September was the signal for Jiang Qing and her associates, the Gang of Four[6] to extend their power. Meanwhile a week's mourning was declared and Mao's body lay in state while 300,000 people filed past. On 18 September Hua delivered the final eulogy at the funeral ceremonies attended by the potential contenders for power. A facade of unity was not preserved for long: on

Figure 8.1 Funeral rally for Mao Zedong, 18 September 1976, with Hua
Guofeng (centre), published in *China Pictorial*, no. 11, 1976, with the
Gang of Four, who by then had been arrested, airbrushed out of the
picture.

6 October Hua gave orders for the arrest of Mao's widow, her three
leading associates and more than twenty others. It was rumoured that
they planned a coup involving the assassination of Hua, and the military leader Ye Jianying with backing from the militia in Shanghai and
other cities. In fact they were ill-prepared and any support they had
quickly evaporated. How far they were really depending on a coup for
their success is questionable. They had not tried to use their power base
in Shanghai but remained in Beijing apparently expecting that their
control of the media and links to Mao could be transformed into political power.

Hua was elevated by a countercoup backed by Ye Jianying and Wang
Dongxing,[7] who was in charge of the Party guard unit '8341'. The decision to arrest the four radical leaders was made in the early morning of
5 October at a meeting of Hua, Ye, Wang, Chen Xilian, commander of
the Beijing garrison and Li Xiannian, ally of Deng Xiaoping. On 10
October it was announced that Hua had been made Chairman of the
Central Committee as well as head of the Military Commission. A
detailed news release of the arrests on 21 October was followed by
organized celebrations all over China. Foreign observers commented
that these rallies reflected genuine popular satisfaction that the Gang of
Four had been brought down.

Although Mao had wanted his remains sent to his home village, Hua
arranged for a mausoleum to be built in Tiananmen Square in order to
put Mao on permanent display. There millions of people have been
able to pay their last respects to the larger than life figure, somewhat

swollen by the embalming fluid. The new leadership continued to invoke Mao on whom the legitimacy of Hua's succession depended. The fact that he had arrested Mao's widow was no great problem, although there was some muttering about the policies of a Gang of Five; the implication being that Mao himself was culpable.

Soon after Hua took office, attempts were made to build up his image, with posters displaying portraits of Hua and Mao side by side and lavish praise of Hua in the press. In February 1977 the *People's Daily* declared, 'We resolutely defend whatever policies Chairman Mao has formulated and unswervingly adhere to whatever instructions Chairman Mao has issued.' Those who adhered to this policy were to be categorized as the 'whateverists'.

By this time there was a growing groundswell in favour of Deng Xiaoping's return to political life. (Since the previous spring, 1976, he had been in Guangzhou protected by the regional military leader, Xu Shiyou.) On the anniversary of Zhou's death in January 1977 crowds came to Tiananmen Square to honour his memory. Among them were supporters of Deng Xiaoping who, along with some posters calling for his return, hung up bottles labelled 'hen hao' (very good): a clearly understood pun since 'xiao ping' (meaning small bottle) sounded like Deng's name. More importantly some members of the Central Committee were pressing for Deng's recall. In July 1977, at the plenum of the Central Committee which confirmed Hua as party leader and the position of Ye Jianying, the military leader, Deng was installed as number three in the Party hierarchy. Some sort of deal had been struck since Hua, having been confirmed as Chairman of the Party and Head of the Military Commission, proposed the restoration of Deng to the positions he had held before his fall in 1976, namely member of the Politburo Standing Committee, Vice-Chairman of the Central Committee, first Deputy Premier of the State Council, Vice-Chairman of the Military Commission and Chief of the General Staff in the People's Liberation Army. It has been suggested that in return Deng promised to support Hua.[8]

The party's Eleventh Congress followed in August. Hua eulogized Mao for the 'successes' of the Cultural Revolution, while condemning the Gang of Four which Mao was credited with having identified as a threat. While it was declared that the Cultural Revolution was officially over, Hua maintained that class struggle as the 'key link' must be maintained. Deng quoted Mao (from 1942) on the importance 'of seeking truth from facts'. Although this slogan was not formally taken up by the Congress, it was to become the watchword of Deng's supporters in their opposition to the 'whateverists'.

The Communist Party had grown. By the Eleventh Congress (August 1977) it had increased to over 35 million members. More than half of them had joined since 1966 and seven million since 1973. With the election of the new Central Committee at the end of the Congress there was a noticeable political shift: about a third of its former members especially those seen as 'Gang of Four' radicals were not re-elected and they were replaced in the main by cadres who were disgraced in the Cultural Revolution but had recently been rehabilitated. Across China in April 1978 more than 100,000 former rightists had the label removed. Those still in prison or exile were set free.

Meanwhile Hua had taken up Zhou Enlai's Four Modernizations and set in train a programme for a ten-year plan. Nominally this was to run from 1976 to 1985. The plan was based on the Stalinist command concept, but was to be financed by foreign capitalists, especially Japan. The plan was published in February 1978 and it very soon became clear that it was not going to achieve its targets. Since China lacked both resources and trained personnel (the Cultural Revolution years had taken their toll), foreign investors were chary.

As intellectuals came back to their work in the cities in 1977–8 so the process of returning education to its pre-Cultural Revolution form continued. The question of restoring entrance examinations had been in the air since 1971–2. The egalitarians had fought a rearguard action to preserve selection by ideology and the importance of red over expert. They lost the battle; by the end of the decade the principle of competitive examination was firmly established and key universities provided a high-flying route for a very small minority.

Under Hua the universities and higher research institutes were revived and acknowledged as a necessary concomitant to the Four Modernizations. Chen Yun, one of the architects of the first five-year plan, 1953–7, reappeared. Hua's government hoped to finance the import of technology with coal and oil exports. More stringent management controls in factories were combined with material incentives. On 1 October 1977 workers in state enterprises had a 10 per cent wage increase, the first significant rise for twenty years. But Hua's reforms, constrained within a command economy, failed to make a breakthrough. The fundamental problem for Hua's leadership was that since it was time for further changes from the commitment politics of the Maoist era to pragmatically determined methods of economic development, the best man for that job was Deng Xiaoping. The real transformation was to come as elements of a free market economy developed in agriculture and industry under the political drive of Deng and his supporters in the 1980s.

President Nixon's visit in 1972 had been slowly followed by the relaxation of travel controls. More and more foreign friendship groups and specialist tourist groups toured China. A growing number of Chinese went abroad to study. Hua's government cited Mao's adage 'Make foreign things serve China'. With official cultural exchanges, the visits of foreign orchestras and translations of Western classics came also the first trickle of popular music from Hong Kong and elsewhere. The plays, films, operas and journals banned during the Cultural Revolution reappeared. A feature of the new literature was short stories by a new generation of writers describing their experiences in the Cultural Revolution.

TURNING POINT

After the Eleventh Party Congress in August 1977 the debate between Hua and Deng intensified. Deng's well-known aphorism 'it doesn't matter what colour the cat is as long as it catches mice'[9] was a direct denial of the Maoist idea that it is 'more important to be red than expert'. By this time the ball was in Deng's hands. Not only had the course of the Cultural Revolution left general disillusionment in its wake but the need for experts to promote modernization was obvious. Moreover, as Maoist self-sufficiency had become redundant with the new opening-up to foreign technical interchange, so the cultural self-sufficiency of Maoism could less easily be justified. In any case, as Deng and his followers could argue, the intellectuals were an integral part of the workforce and no conflict could or should exist between mental and manual workers.

From maintaining the need to 'seek truth from facts' Deng went on to stress the importance of practice : after all Mao himself had said that 'correct ideas come from social practice and it alone'. Deng's argument was aired in the press in May and by him in a speech to the All Army Conference on Political Work on 2 June. On 1 July a speech given by Mao in January 1964 was republished prominently (originally it had appeared in the Red Guard press.) It was a reminder that not only had Mao at that time spoken of the need for collective leadership, he had also confessed to errors he had committed during the Great Leap Forward. This concept of a fallible Mao made nonsense of the whateverists' argument that his teachings should be the absolute criteria for truth.

In the second part of 1978 the matter was argued out in party meetings up and down the country. The 'whateverists' had the support of many cadres who feared for their positions if there were a general reappraisal of the past. Apart from the two main sides there was also the 'wind faction', so-called because it consisted of those who 'trim their sails according to the wind'.

A Central Committee work conference (9 November to 13 December) was followed by the Third Plenum of the Central Committee. The outcome was a decisive victory for Deng's views. Class struggle as the key link' was dropped. Peng Dehuai (posthumously) and others who had been condemned under Mao were exonerated. (It was thought better to leave the case of Liu Shaoqi for the time being). There was also the matter of the 1976 Tiananmen Memorial Incident, when Deng had been demoted. This had been dealt with at the work conference and the decision to rehabilitate those who had suffered was confirmed at the Third Plenum. Since Hua, as acting Premier and Minister of Public Security had had a well-known part in the original proceedings, the reassessment was not good for his image.

In fact from the Third Plenum on, Hua's days were numbered. It was later revealed that a section of the leadership under Deng decided he would have to go. There was no unseemly haste. While Deng's associates Hu Yaobang, Deng Yingzhao and Wang Zhen joined the Politburo, Chen Yun was promoted to the Standing Committee and given responsibility for Party discipline, Hua maintained a high profile in the press and at formal functions dealing with foreign dignitaries, for example.

THE RISE AND FALL OF DEMOCRACY WALL

During the winter of 1978–9 the political changes at the top coincided with an upsurge of protest from below, particularly by young workers, a phenomenon known as Democracy Wall. Wall posters expressing free and frank political comment appeared on a stretch of wall in the centre of Beijing not far from government offices in the Forbidden City. The posters were followed by the publication of magazines, pamphlets and booklets. The authors were inspired partly by the recent opening up to the West and were also encouraged by the new verdict on the 1976 demonstration. The gist of many of the writings was to blame Mao as in:

> Chairman's tomb and Emperor's palace
> face each other across the square,
> One great leader in his wisdom
> made our countless futures bare, . . .

and to praise Deng as in:

Wise and talented, like the Duke of Zhou,
he's Hua's right hand.
He'll chat and laugh easily, and by lifting a finger
make people and country happy and peaceful.[10]

It seems to have suited Deng to appear to go along with the early manifestations of this populism.

A famous poster put up on 5 December 1978 by a young man Wei Jingsheng[11] was headed 'The Fifth Modernization'. By this he meant democracy; 'the right of the people to choose their own representatives'. He added 'the people must have the power to replace their representatives any time so that these representatives cannot go on deceiving others in the name of the people.'[12] In December and January there were also demonstrations by people who had been sent to the countryside, who wished to be rehabilitated. An estimated 30,000 workers with their families installed themselves in the centre of Beijing and appealed for government help. Some died of the cold. There were also protests in Shanghai, Guangzhou and Hangzhou.

However, in the spring of 1979 the regime took steps to suppress this developing movement with its appeals for human rights and democracy. Within two weeks of China's withdrawal from its military incursion into Vietnam (see Chapter 7) Wei Jingsheng had been arrested. He had compounded his challenge to the Party by criticizing Deng's insensitivity and also exposing conditions in China's political prisons. He was also accused of treasonably giving information on the Sino-Vietnam War to a foreign journalist. He was sentenced to fifteen years imprisonment. As for the Democracy Wall, by April the brief freedom of expression was over; posters were allowed only under police supervision and Democracy Wall closed down in December.

CLOSING THE CULTURAL REVOLUTION

By 1979 it was becoming clear that the economic programme presented as the Ten-Year Plan in February 1978 was not going to work. It had been based on an unrealistic assessment of the conditions in China. The Central Committee work conference in April 1979 laid down the lines of a policy of retrenchment and reform. Retrenchment involved the cancellation of contracts already signed with foreign companies and payment of compensation in convertible funds which China could ill-afford. Reform required: readjustment, restructuring, consolidation and improvement. Imbalances in the economy would be adjusted, economic management would be restructured; enterprises would be reorganized to increase efficiency and the quality of production, technology and management was to be improved.

A positive development was a new approach to the production of reliable data. In place of the fudged semi-secret accounting of earlier eras, reliable statistics were published in which one year could be compared with the next; a practice which has been maintained since.

By February 1980 at the Fifth Plenum there were further political changes. A restored Secretariat of eleven members, responsible to the Standing Committee of the Politburo was set up to oversee the activities of the Central Committee. Hu Yaobang was made general secretary of this body. Hu and Zhao Ziyang joined the Standing Committee of the Politburo while four former members who were deemed 'whateverists' were demoted.

The plenum was a political milestone; it finally faced up to the question of Liu Shaoqi. He was declared to be a great Marxist and proletarian revolutionary and one of the principal leaders of the Party and the State. After a decade of vilification – during which no speech was complete without ritual denunciation – it was now officially declared that 'the labels of renegade, traitor and scab' should be removed. Deng recognized that this could lead to 'considerable ideological confusion' and at a memorial meeting on 17 May Deng himself delivered the eulogy.

The credibility of the Communist Party was being tested and it was now an appropriate time for historical reassessment. Meetings to prepare a 'resolution on certain questions in the history of our Party since the foundation of the People's Republic of China' commenced in spring 1980 and was completed by June 1981. In the meantime a trial was staged for the Gang of Four (arrested in 1976) and some of their associates. It began on 20 November 1980 and the verdicts were given on 25 January 1981.

It was claimed that a salient feature of the trial 'was the clear separation of what was legally criminal from what was political'.[13] At the same time the trial was intended to sum up the political errors of the Cultural Revolution. The accused were the 'Lin Biao and Jiang Qing' cliques, conveniently linked as having perpetrated crimes while attempting to extend their powers. They were disassociated from Mao. The analogy given by one of the judges (Fei Xiaotong, Director of the Institute of Sociology, Chinese Academy of Social Sciences) was that the navigator, Mao, of a liner, China, speeding along a course, socialism, made an error and entered dangerous waters. At that point some of the crew conspired to seize control of the ship, committing murder and other foul crimes in the process.[14]

There were ten 'culprits' in the dock: the 'Gang of Four', Jiang Qing, Zhang Chunqiao, Yao Wenyuan and Wang Hongwen; five of Lin Biao's generals, plus Chen Boda.[15] The millions of Chinese who followed the proceedings on radio, television and in the press may well have been impressed by the judicial proceedings which 'made a tremendous impact in a country lacking in a tradition of rule by law.'[16] To westerners it smacked of a political trial with preordained verdicts. All the accused confessed except Zhang Chunqiao, who refused to acknowledge the tribunal and Jiang Qing, who made a spirited defence. 'I was Chairman Mao's dog. Whomever he told me to bite, I bit.' When she scorned the court 'In the war years, I was the only woman with Chairman Mao at the front. Where were you hiding then?' the handpicked audience of 1,200 laughed, possibly with embarrassment – one of the few spontaneous moments of the trial. Jiang Qing and Zhang Chunqiao were given death sentences postponed for two years, and then commuted indefinitely; the others were sentenced to long terms of imprisonment, Wang Hongwen for life. Chen Boda and the generals were released on grounds of failing health. Jiang Qing, who was said to spend her time making dolls, reportedly committed suicide in 1991.

The trial had served to write a line under the Cultural Revolution. It had circumvented the awkward question of explaining what Mao had actually done. From now on Mao – at least in his post-Liberation period – was presented as less than perfect. Trained guides talking to foreign visitors compared Mao to Churchill, with a better reputation in war than peacetime. The trial was the forerunner for less publicized trials throughout China of other 'followers of the Gang of Four'.

The role of Mao was faced squarely when the Resolution on Party History, adopted in June 1981, became required reading for 39 million members of the CCP, clearing the way for a new era. The Resolution maintained that notwithstanding Mao's mistakes he was 'a great proletarian revolutionary' who had paid 'constant attention to overcoming shortcomings'. As for 'the system of Mao Zedong thought' this was held to be 'the crystallization of the collective wisdom of the CCP'. The verdict on the Cultural Revolution was a 'comprehensive long drawn out and grave blunder,' a 'tremendous misfortune for the Party and the people'. Now that the CCP had the 'courage to acknowledge and correct its mistakes' the way was clear to face the tasks of turning China into a modern socialist country. Much discussion, soul-searching and compromise went into producing the final document. Deng considered that on the whole it was 'a balanced appraisal'.[17]

The transfer of power was about to be completed. The sixth plenum of the Central Committee, which adopted the Resolution on 27 June

1981, also accepted Hua's resignation from the chairmanship of the CC and the military affairs commission. Deng Xiaoping took the military post and Hu Yaobang the political.[18] Hu accepting his promotion at the sixth plenum had averred that he would continue to need guidance from the four[19] party elders on the Standing Committee and in particular Deng Xiaoping 'the primary decision maker in the CCP today'.[20]

9 'Socialism with Chinese characteristics', 1981–9

Deng's Xiaoping's era has seen the unprecedented opening-up of Communist China. Since the later nineteenth century China had been subject to increasing western influences, particularly under the GMD regime. But after 1949 the circumstances of the Cold War tended to isolate China from the world economy, and Maoist introspection, if for a time it tolerated Soviet Russian ideas, did not welcome Western thought. Both as proud nationalists and as ideological flag bearers in the 1950s and 1960s the Chinese saw virtue as the reward for the necessity of being self-reliant. This was in contrast to the other developing countries which had the benefits and disadvantages of being economically tied to the developed world often in a colonial, post-colonial or neo-colonial relationship. With the ending of the Cultural Revolution it fell eventually to the Dengists to oversee a wide and growing interaction with the rest of the world. Economic growth led to a political problem. In place of the economic dead end of Maoism there arose the contradiction between international mores – the rule of law and democracy – and the totalitarian traditions of the Communist party, determined to maintain stability by enforcing conformity. Democracy was arguably too novel in China to be absorbed painlessly if at all. It has caused a big question mark to hang over Deng's regime.

It was Deng above all others who masterminded China's remarkable development in the 1980s. Was he driven by principles he had held long and consistently? For much of his career he was a loyal and respected follower of Mao but he appears less ideologically dogmatic in his commitment to communism than many other Party leaders. He has a reputation for pragmatism but it would be misleading to describe him as just a pragmatist. He was a revolutionary whose commitment to modernization was linked to the pursuit of economic growth by which living standards would rise. 'Poverty is not socialism' he said in 1987. Unlike China's previous leaders, Mao and Hua, he shunned cult status. From about 1980 until his death in 1997 he was recognized as China's 'paramount leader'. He chaired the Military Affairs Commission from 1981 but the top political posts were often held by others. By elevating his protégés, Hu Yaobang and Zhao Ziyang in 1981, he was taking steps, which Mao had failed to do, to provide for political succession.

THE RESPONSIBILITY SYSTEM

Foreigners visiting China in 1981 were told that an experiment was taking place in the countryside. It was arranged for them to visit two communes only a few miles apart. At the first, the members of a production team were preparing a rice paddy with seed, fertilizer and bird repellent for which they were credited with work-points. At the second the visitors were introduced to a new 'responsibility system' in which families entered into a temporary contract to produce a quota of grain, after which they made a profit for themselves.

The principle of the responsibility system had been formally approved in December 1978. The land, which continued to be held by the state, was worked by the contracting household which made decisions on planting and cultivation and the timetabling of their labour. By 1984 the 'experimental' system had become standard all over the country and some contracts were being extended for fifteen years. The outcome was a remarkable increase in productivity, not only of the basic grain crops but also in sideline activities, for example weaving straw mats and raising rabbits, and in rural industries, such as refining grains, which by the end of 1985 amounted to 66 per cent of the value of rural production. Family cultivation did not apparently inhibit mechanization. Tractors were hired or bought; by 1984 individual households had the use of more than 90 per cent of China's tractors. So energetically did the peasants take their new responsibilities that by rescheduling the time spent on basic crop production they found much more time for ancillary activities. In fact so successful were the new endeavours in the countryside that by 1984 there was too much grain to be stored properly. When the government reduced the rate paid for the grain quota, the peasants reacted by spending more time producing cash crops and other products for market. The new opportunities in the countryside have had implications for the status of the villagers; a change acknowledged by those writers who now refer to farmers rather than peasants.

Free enterprise received approving headlines in the press. 'Prosperous

Girls Attract Husbands' announced the Shanghai *Wenhui Bao*[1] explaining how a group of peasant spinsters from a village in Jiangsu, having made money under the responsibility system, were wooed by young men working in a nearby factory.

By 1987 the right to use plots of land could be bought and sold. The commune in its controlling role had become redundant. The market towns and villages were no longer subject to the planned economy of the commune system.

INDUSTRIAL EXPANSION

How was industry to break away from the Stalinist command economy? In the early 1980s the production increase per head was only 10 per cent up on the early 1950s. In the absence of market forces there was the problem of devising production strategies and setting quotas. What stimulus would best encourage management and workers? The Daqing model of heroic endeavour for the sake of the enterprise was still being invoked by Hua in the late 1970s; but it did not offer a way out of the straitjacket of central control.

State control could not easily be abandoned. Whereas in the countryside it was relatively easy to use local resources to provide capital for improving farms, the provision of capital for factory development needed to be on a larger scale. Meanwhile China's leaders hesitated to introduce a stock exchange and merchant banks to raise capital. The early experiments with joint foreign enterprises had mixed success (see Chapter 8).

As in the case of agriculture, industrial reforms beginning in 1979 were first tried out locally, for example, in Sichuan (the province Deng Xiaoping came from). A factory would agree to produce a quota of goods at a fixed price and could sell any surplus at a profit on the open market. The management had some discretion in using the profit for reinvestment in the factory or for the welfare of its workers. Individuals were rewarded with wage increases and bonuses.

By 1982 all government controlled industry had a measure of self-dependence. While there was an increase in production, e.g. in rolled steel products from 2.2 million tonnes in 1978 to 2.9 million tonnes in 1982, there were new problems. As funds were retained locally, the centre lost revenue. Moreover, some factories which increased production nevertheless had overall losses because of bad management, unimproved plant or bad luck. As a next stage, in 1983 and 1984 the government sought to extend local responsibility while maintaining and even increasing taxation. Although this could account for 85 per cent of the profits, the enterprise was allowed to keep the 15 per cent surplus.

As in the countryside, small enterprises in the cities requiring less capital were relatively more profitable. This was where the enthusiastic small entrepreneurial family came into its own; the figures show 100,000 private businesses registered in 1978, 6 million in 1983 and 17 million in 1985.[2]

It was not going to be easy for China to modernize effectively and quickly using only internal resources. What were the prospects for foreign trade and investment? In 1959 the value of China's foreign trade was $4.4 billion; in 1970 $4.6 billion. After the Nixon visit it grew rapidly to $15 billion in the mid-1970s and to $38 billion by 1980. Negative trade balances in 1974–5 and 1978–80 had led to the abandonment of some projects but in 1981 the balance of exports over imports began to rise, partly through tourism and the sale of arms to the Middle East. Efforts to promote trade included increasing the number of trade fairs, for long limited to an annual event in Guangzhou.

SPECIAL ECONOMIC ZONES

One scheme to attract foreign capital and to bring in new technology was the setting-up in 1979 of special zones separate from the rest of the country in the coastal regions of south China at Shenzhen, Zhuhai, Shantou and Xiamen. With an improved infrastructure (of roads, power supplies and port facilities) provided by the government at significant expense, foreign enterprises were encouraged to take advantage of a cheap labour force. The production and management skills thus acquired would in theory benefit the country as a whole.

The special economic zones had a fair measure of success but were not without problems: the technology which was introduced was not necessarily the most advanced since the workforce and the facilities available, although of a higher level than in the rest of China, were not as high as in Hong Kong and Taiwan, so foreign firms have tended to use the zones as places where secondary work can be performed by cheap labour; also, while workers inside the zones have benefited, their experience has not been easily transferred to the rest of the country; moreover, much of the production of the zones has been sold in China. As for the balance of trade, foreign imports were much greater than exports in some years.

The principle of selectively opening up has been extended. For example in 1984 the island province of Hainan[3] and fourteen coastal cities were promoted with tax incentives for foreigners. This evolved into a coastal development plan encompassing the areas of Guangzhou, Xiamen, Shanghai and Lüda (Dalian) (estuaries of Pearl, Min and Yangzi rivers) on Liaoning peninsula. By 1988 288 counties in eleven provinces were declared open. In addition to official activity business men in Hong Kong and Taiwan invested in local enterprises informally through family and village contacts.

The economic changes in the coastal areas which were visibly benefiting the people of the regions created a marked distinction from the interior of the country. This led to the criticism that the zones were similar to the nineteenth century treaty ports, where a few Chinese had benefited from proximity to privileged foreigners.[4] At the frontier of economic development Hainan island saw much tricky and dubious enterprise; for example the import of duty free vehicles which were improperly sent on to the mainland led to the dismissal of the island's Governor Lei Yu in 1985.[5] Hainan at the time also became a by-word for corruption and embezzlement, and notorious for its flourishing casinos and brothels. Not for nothing did Deng's lieutenant Zhu Rongji, visiting in 1992, describe Hainan as a 'Special Economic Zone with Hainan characteristics'.[6]

An American observer of the changes in China over many years offers a new version of Deng's famous phrase: 'It doesn't matter whether the cat is black or white, it doesn't even matter whether the cat can catch mice. What matters is that the cat does not get caught.'[7]

LAW

In 1949 the Communist government declared that the Guomindang laws were no longer valid. Processes for drawing up new legal codes were interrupted by the Great Leap Forward. Most legal experts in government offices lost their jobs in the anti-rightist crackdown in 1957 and the Ministry of Justice was abolished in 1959. Thereafter China was governed not by a code of laws but by decrees, bureaucratic regulations and official orders. These were available in government offices, but many of them were not published.[8]

By the late 1970s foreigners considering investment in China, not least the legalistically minded Americans, were asking for laws governing contract, property, taxation, etc., which would make their position in China more predictable.[9]

In March 1979 a planning conference following the guideline of the third plenum of the Eleventh Central Committee stressed the importance of international law. A start was made in September when students were admitted to Beijing University to study International Law; articles were published and in 1981 a textbook of international law was published. (Meanwhile China was admitted to the International Monetary Fund and the World Bank[10]). This was only the beginning, but at least some of the bureaucratic regulations were made clearer. The importance of recruiting legal personnel was recognized. In 1982 the Ministry of Justice accepted over 50,000 'outstanding army officers' transferred from the army for retraining for legal work. This expedient was not enough; by 1993 it was announced that there were only 50,000 lawyers and another 100,000 would be trained by the end of the century.

The new constitution passed by the Twelfth Congress in 1982 laid down that the Party must act 'within the limits permitted by the Constitution and the laws of the state.' Hu Yaobang explained that no one 'from the Central Committee down to the grass roots (was) to act in contravention of the Constitution and the laws.'[11]

The importance of 'an all-inclusive legal system' to the 'establishment and improvement of the socialist market economic structure' was recognized in the Decision of the CCP Central Committee on Some Issues . . ., 14 November 1993. Effective law enforcement should combat corruption, tax avoidance, 'guarantee economic growth and safeguard the legitimate rights and interests of the citizen'. It was felt necessary to state that administrators were not above the law, i.e. 'Governments at various levels should abide by law in administrative matters'.[12] Such expressed intentions have not meant that it has been accepted that the will of the Party should be hampered by ideas of fundamental rights. The problem of reconciling the concept of an independent judiciary with an all-powerful party remains.

'TO GET RICH IS GLORIOUS'

The new economic policies brought problems that were both inherent and ancillary. An inherent problem was that incentives for hard work and skill led to greater social inequality. At the same time economic flexibility was not compatible with job security – 'the iron ricebowl' – and the system of welfare provision by one's work unit was undermined. Individuals could move around more easily. Previously they were only able to use their food coupons in their officially registered place of residence or buy food on the free market. Now they could

公用电话

Figure 9.1 'Many people make calls to judicial organs to report officials who commit economic crimes.' An offence-reporting system was set up in June 1988 with over 5,000 hotlines. It was described in an illustrated article in *Beijing Review*, 15–21 January 1990.

travel from village to town and city to city looking for work. Unofficial informal labour exchanges operated on street corners and in parks. The supply of food and clothing hitherto limited by coupons became more expensive in a market economy. With the decline of the welfare services (including medical care) provided by the factory or commune, individuals and families have had to fall back on their own resources.

One apparently unforeseen problem which emerged was posed by the unresolved status of all those who at Mao's behest had been sent to the countryside. Forbidden to return home to the cities, some of them had become attached to the communes. Many, however, lacked the farming skills of peasants born in the country and because of their uncertain status they had not easily found wives. Now there was no longer a minimum grain allowance for all those living in a rural community. In April 1985 claiming to represent 20,000 exiles in Shaanxi, hundreds made their way to Beijing and sat in protest on the steps of the communist party headquarters. Although not badly treated for this illegal demonstration, they failed to get reassurance that they would be rehabilitated. The same problem was faced in other provinces and by many people. There were in any case long waiting lists for accommodation in the cities.

The reforms led to a general rise in living standards but also to increasing inequality in the workforce and growing regional disparities. Western-style consumer goods became more widely available, but at the same time there was growing unemployment and beggars appeared on the streets.

The negative social consequences of reform, and the question of speed of change, were at the heart of the intra-Party debate. This is sometimes portrayed – at risk of oversimplification – as between the moderate reformers and those who favoured radical change in spite of the problems that went with it, the 'bold' reformers.

The ancillary problems were another matter. Both categories of reformers recognized these even if they did not agree on how to deal with them. There was corruption, sometimes believed to be inevitable in any period of pioneering entrepreneurial expansion. But bribes to smooth the transaction of business are one thing; extortion by the Party secretary whether in factory or village is another. The power of these men has enabled them to make and break contracts, practise nepotism and get rich ingloriously! To such men the factory or the village is a fief. As the historian Jack Gray remarks, 'When Chinese dissenters claim that Chinese socialism is a form of feudalism they know whereof they speak.'[13]

Moreover there was the phenomenon described as 'opening the window lets in the flies'. Contact with the west brought 'spiritual pollution'; at one level a questioning of the omnipotence of the Party or riotously 'bourgeois' pop music, or at its worst a culture of crime, prostitution and drugs.

This has fuelled the debate. For example in 1984 the 'virtue' of getting rich reached an apogee when the Party secretary of Guangdong province said 'the more revolution you make, the richer you should become.'[14] Then in 1985 it was asserted that the concept 'money is above everything' was wrong. The debate continues. It is only peripherally related to the question of democracy but cannot be uncoupled from Western modernization. For example in 1983 the attack on spiritual pollution including pornography, modern fashion and individualistic literary values was ordered to be played down by Deng's government when it threatened to lead to the rejection of all Western ideas including essential new technology. But by 1986 the conservatives in the Party were focusing their criticism on 'bourgeois liberalization'.

In December 1986 there were notable student demonstrations at the key university of Science and Technology at Hefei in Anhui. The vice-president of the university, distinguished astro-physicist Fang Lizhi[15] had been arguing for complete westernization. He maintained that China was not partially backward and in need of piecemeal reforms; China was backward 'in all respects' and it was ridiculous to talk of building socialism or anything else with Chinese characteristics. Chinese modernization would be a contradiction in terms – what China needed was 'complete' modernization. To this, Party old timer Bo Yibo retorted 'We must not think that the moon in foreign countries is fuller than in China.'[16]

It is apparent that China was experiencing a recurring pattern of relaxation and control. This was identified as a fang-shou cycle which was seen to occur three times in the 1980s.[17] Economic liberalisation and an increase in the tolerated intellectual freedom created perceived disorder and led to a conservative backlash. Was this inevitable? Were the contradictions inherent in China's change irreconcilable? It may be seen to Deng's credit that he did not think so, that he believed that speeding up and slowing down the rate of change would in effect define a middle channel through which China could be safely steered. If stern measures were necessary to hold the banks against the oscillating current, so be it; there could be no uncontrolled flood.

The relatively permissive atmosphere following the replacement of Party propaganda chief Deng Liqun by Zhu Houze and the appointment of a new Minister of Culture, the writer Wang Meng, in the summer of 1985 had seen something of an artistic, theatrical, and cinematic renaissance. There were new academic and professional societies, new journals e.g. *World Economic Herald* and the upward trend of the intelligentsia seemed assured.

The mounting student disturbances towards the end of 1986 culminated in the public burning of the *Beijing Daily* on 5 January 1987. Already on 30 December Deng Xiaoping had made a statement 'On the problem of the present student disturbances'. He said:

> We do all we can to avoid bloodshed. If not even a single person dies, that is the best way. It is even preferable to allow our own people to be injured. If we do not take appropriate steps and measures, we will be unable to control this type of incident; if we pull

back we will encounter even more trouble later on . . . Don't worry that foreigners will say we have ruined our reputation . . . we must show foreigners that the political situation in China is stable.

Deng lashed out at Fang Lizhi. He condemned ideas of bourgeois democracy. 'We cannot set up such gimmicks as the division of powers between three branches of government. This causes great trouble.' Citing the Polish government's handling of the Solidarity confrontation in 1981, he said, 'This proves that you cannot succeed without recourse to methods of dictatorship.'[18]

In general the reaction was sternly avuncular rather than vicious. Vice-Premier Li Peng called for curriculum changes in schools and colleges and henceforth the criteria for admission to middle school and university would include political attitudes.

CHANGES IN THE LEADERSHIP

Deng's protégés and presumed successors Zhao Ziyang, Premier and Hu Yaobang, General Secretary of the Party had joined the Standing Committee of the Politburo in 1982. Some who were opposed to the pace of reform, notably Peng Zhen and Chen Yun, fought a rearguard action but – with the backing of paramount leader Deng – Hu and Zhao presided effectively and with some skill during a time of great change. Zhao went some way to shaking up the state bureaucracies replacing old cadres and restructuring the State Council. He gave more scope to the experts who produced reports for new policy study groups.

Hu Yaobang made a good impression when he visited London in June 1986. His suit and tie were well up to the standard of Chatham House when he addressed the Royal Institute of International Affairs. Asked whether the trends in westernization and liberalization would continue, he replied boldly – Yes. There might be some slowing down but there would be no reversal of current policies. However, it was his fate to be held responsible for the 1986 student demonstrations. By then he had declined in favour with Deng Xiaoping, allegedly for presuming upon his succession. Having been asked three times to resign Hu was dismissed from his post as General Secretary on 16 January 1987. The document (Central Document no 3 1987) listed his wrongdoing which included [politically] 'only opposing the "Left"' while 'never opposing the "Right"', [economically] putting too much emphasis on consumer demand and [in foreign relations] saying 'many things he should not have said.' Hu certainly appeared to take acceptance of westernization to the limit. A more cautious politician might not have proposed that chopsticks should be given up in favour of knives and forks which were more hygienic. The same document included Hu's confession in which he admitted that 'his ideological laxity had fostered spiritual pollution and bourgeois liberalization, thereby bringing on student turmoil'.[19] He was allowed to stay in the Politburo.

Zhao Ziyang succeeded Hu Yaobang as (acting) General Secretary. At the Thirteenth Party Congress in October–November 1987 Deng retained his authority – the Central Committee secretly agreed that he should remain the paramount leader to be consulted on all major decisions – and he remained Chairman of the Military Affairs Committee. Chen Yun, became Chairman of the Central Advisory Commission and General Secretary of the Central Discipline Inspection Commission. Li Peng became a member of the five-man Standing Committee of the Politburo; in April 1988 at the Seventh National People's Congress he became Premier. Yang Shangkun succeeded Li Xiannian as President of the People's Republic.[20]

Throughout 1988, in spite of the efforts of the conservatives, a groundswell of discontent, particularly among students, persisted. Yet it was a relatively quiet year. There was some concern over inflation and other aspects of the economy; as a result Zhao Ziyang handed many of his economic responsibilities over to Li Peng.

1989

1989 was the fortieth anniversary of Communist China. It was to be a fateful year; noted by some intellectuals as the bicentenary of the French Revolution in 1789, it was also the seventieth anniversary of 4 May 1919 when student demonstrations signalled the intellectual turning point for modern China. To mark the occasion Fang Lizhi sent an open letter to Deng Xiaoping proposing an amnesty for political prisoners including Wei Jingsheng on 4 May 1989. Other leading intellectuals in China supported this suggestion which was taken up as a human rights concern around the world. Meanwhile Party conservatives, notably Chen Yun and Bo Yibo, were calling for the replacement of Zhao Ziyang. Deng was not convinced that now Hu had gone he needed to replace yet another of his trusted lieutenants. He decided to postpone the matter until after the planned visit of Mikhail Gorbachev, still riding high on his policies of glasnost and perestroika.

Then on 8 April Hu Yaobang, having made a speech to an enlarged meeting of the Politburo calling for the Party to increase its support for education, had a heart attack and died a week later. One rumour had it that he had collapsed while battling verbally with Bo Yibo. In any case his death provided the occasion for a popular display of political grief (akin to the 1976 incident in memory of Zhou Enlai.) At first hundreds, then within a few days tens of thousands, of students marched to Tiananmen Square. The student protest organization at Beijing University set out their demands addressed to the NPC Standing Committee. Just as Hu had been made to take responsibility for the 1986 student protests so the students now called for the 'correct evaluation' of Hu as the centrepiece of their demands for reforms; these included rehabilitation for those victimized, freedom of the press, publication of the salaries and other incomes of the top leaders and better remuneration for teachers and students. By the day of the official memorial service for Hu Yaobang, 22 April, feelings were running high but brawls between students and police were minimal. On the same day at a meeting of the Politburo it was decided not to give way to student demands; the next day Zhao Ziyang left Beijing for a planned visit to North Korea. In his absence a meeting of the Standing Committee convened by Li Peng, the Premier, decided to take a strong line against 'an extremely small number of people' whose goal 'was a planned conspiracy, a riot, whose real nature was to fundamentally negate the leadership of the Chinese Communist Party and to negate the socialist system.'[21]

Li Peng had good reason for concern: the students were bent on further confrontation. On 27 April more than 50,000 students with a large number of workers alongside paraded for thirty miles through Beijing. The rows of policemen and soldiers lined up to stop them were brushed aside.

The students were still confident. They sang the Internationale and chanted slogans, calling for the support of 'correct leadership'. The authorities agreed to meet student leaders for discussion. Zhao Ziyang and some others in the government may genuinely have hoped that the conflict could be resolved by dialogue. But the students were set for another major demonstration on 4 May. While Zhao appalled Party conservatives by stating: 'The students' demands for correcting errors so as to march forward coincide with those of the Party and the government', the protest was spreading to other major cities. In Beijing journalists began to organize a movement for freedom of the press.

The devices employed by the students included a bicycle cavalcade, which did not work well, and a hunger strike, which was very effective in generating public sympathy. When the General Secretary of the Soviet Union arrived, on what was to have been an historic summit meeting which would recement relations and redound to the credit of Deng's leadership, he could not get to the Great Hall of the People since Tiananmen Square was packed with a massive array of banners, tents, demonstrators including hunger strikers and the world's press. By this time it was not clear what reasonable concessions would have satisfied the students. Nevertheless Zhao Ziyang still hoped conciliation would get a response. His time was running out. When he tried to hand in his resignation, Deng refused to accept it because it would encourage the demonstrators. On 18 May the Politburo Standing Committee, four to one, decided to impose martial law. A dispirited Zhao, his career ended, went late at night to speak to the hunger strikers 'We were too late coming. I'm sorry. Your criticism of us is justified . . . The channels for dialogue are wide open. It could become too late if you insist on getting a satisfactory answer now.' His rambling words were caught on television. Within twenty-four hours soldiers were marching into Beijing.

The demonstration was to be played out for two more weeks. The troops benignly allowed themselves to be held at bay by Beijing citizens, men, women and children, who swarmed in the streets and put up road blocks. The authorities made propaganda counterattacks. Big banners proclaimed 'Maintain Order in the Capital.' On 23 May the troops were moved to the outskirts of the city. Momentarily there was the notion of convening a special meeting of the National People's Congress Standing Committee to bring martial law to an end and dismiss Li Peng. It happened that Wan Li, the chairman of the NPC Standing Committee, was visiting Canada at this time and had remarked to the press that he intended to 'firmly protect the patriotic enthusiasm of the young people in China'. The pro-democracy elements had high hopes for his return. However, Wan Li was nobbled when he touched down in Shanghai; party officials picked him up at the airport and within three days he announced his support for the maintenance of order.

A bizarre turn on 30 May was the erection by art students of a white plaster and polystyrene statue directly opposite Mao's portrait at the north side of Tiananmen Square. As a woman holding a torch it looked something like the Statue of Liberty and was entitled variously as Goddess of Democracy and Spirit of Liberty. It was of course anathema to the regime, at best a childish talisman of how far China's young people had been allowed to wander down a path they did not understand, at worst it was a foreign image 'an insult to our national dignity' said a TV announcer.[22]

Meanwhile arrests had begun starting with three workers, members of the Beijing Autonomous Workers Federation. Traditionally China's authorities have treated students more leniently than other social groups. In this case the sudden emergence of the workers' movement must have seemed to Deng nightmarishly similar to the rise of Solidarity in Poland. Perhaps this is a key to understanding what happened next. On 3 June soon after midnight a column of unarmed troops ran into Tiananmen Square where they were surrounded, immobilized and admonished by a large crowd.[23] In the afternoon thousands of troops came out of underground tunnels behind the Great Hall of the People. They too were surrounded by massed citizenry while student marshals called for discipline and violence was limited. Elsewhere, particularly west of Tiananmen on Changan Avenue, the security forces attacked and ruthlessly dispersed the crowds. Official broadcasts on radio and TV warned people to keep off the streets otherwise they would be 'responsible for their own fate' At 10 p.m. crack troops waiting on the outskirts of the city received their orders to clear Tiananmen Square by 6 a.m. on 4 June.

There was considerable bloodshed, mostly of Beijing residents: estimates vary between 600 and 1,200 dead (and between 6,000 and 10,000 injured) including soldiers. Most of the students in the square after some bickering withdrew quietly. However, there was much confusion and shooting particularly outside the square. At least 39 students died as well as several dozen soldiers, but it would be misleading to describe the events in Beijing that night as simply a 'massacre of students in Tienanmen square'.[24] The crackdown had been concentrated on the civilian masses – an emerging force which could least of all be tolerated if the regime was to survive.

Why had the authorities failed to deal effectively with the demonstration at an earlier stage? Why had the situation been allowed to deteriorate until it was finally dealt with so drastically?

There was disagreement in the leadership combined perhaps with hopes that the protest would peter out. However, by appearing for a time to be willing to listen to the students the Party encouraged bolder activists to press their demands. Within the student leadership the initiative was taken and held by a hard-line group. By this time the mounting discontent could not be appeased. While centring on corruption, and undefined notions of democracy as exemplified by the Spirit of Liberty, the student demands for freedom were essentially a protest against the bureaucratic controls as well as the 'backdoor' practices which circumscribed their education, job prospects, right to travel. They yearned for opportunities to enjoy a wider world of westernization which could hardly be realized under an oppressive and corrupt regime.

Even more irreconcilable were the demands of the marching workers, who since the arrests of workers' leaders on 29 May were gaining support. The discontent of the workers' associations arose out of the economic reforms – the end of jobs for life, the whittling away of welfare provision, the growing gap between rich and poor. Many felt they were losing what they had gained under state socialism. Their demands challenged the basis of Deng's revolution. Was it so surprising that in the end Deng decided to crack down so ruthlessly?

REVERBERATIONS

The media had focused on Tiananmen Square. One immediate reaction was the outburst of demonstrations in Shanghai, Shenyang, Harbin, Changchun, Xian, Guangzhou, Nanjing, Wuhan and other cities across China. Throughout the world there were manifestations of shock and horror and also calls for economic and political retaliation. Even as the Chinese authorities hunted and arrested dissidents, some of the activists managed to escape, smuggled by underground routes to Hong Kong and elsewhere.

Deng Xiaoping appeared on television on 9 June with Li Peng, Peng Zhen, Bo Yibo and other leaders to congratulate the security forces and the military for dealing with a situation caused by the 'handful of bad people' . . . 'the dregs of society'.[25] The aim of these troublemakers 'was to overthrow the Communist Party and the Socialist system' and 'establish a bourgeois republic entirely dependent on the West'. He added ambiguously 'This disturbance was independent of man's will' and 'prompts us to think soberly about the past and will make our steps faster and stronger in the future'.[26] It had necessarily been suppressed but this did not mean that the open door should be closed. On the contrary Deng reiterated his commitment to achieving economic growth which would double the gross national product in twelve years.

Nor in spite of talk of economic sanctions, cutting off investments and credits, by, for example, President Bush was there any consistent effort to put pressure on China.

One outcome of the Tiananmen Crisis was to bring together a group of (formally retired) octogenarians – Deng Xiaoping, Chen Yun, Yang Shangkun, Wang Zhen and Li Xiannian. They ensured the continuance in office of Premier Li Peng. In place of General Secretary Zhao Ziyang (dismissed on 19 May when martial law was declared), they appointed Jiang Zemin, who by 1994 also held the posts of Chairman of the CCP

Military Affairs Commission and President of the PRC. They took steps towards economic retrenchment by giving approval to austerity measures from the centre. The limitation of imports and an export drive, combined with good harvests in 1989 and 1990 brought down inflation.

The differences between Deng and Chen Yun on reform remained: Chen Yun led the conservatives who favoured more government controls, limited international access and a slower growth rate. Deng and his protégés, such as Zhu Rongji former mayor of Shanghai who became vice-premier, believed in more radical reforms emphasizing the market economy, encouraging international economic links and a high growth rate. In January and February 1992 to underline his faith in ongoing economic reforms Deng aged 88 made a 'southern journey' to the Shenzen economic zone and other parts of Guangdong province, extolling the virtues of the open door policy which included large tax incentives for foreign investment and proposing that these should be extended throughout China. Thereafter little was seen of the seriously ageing Deng although his aura remained.

ONE COUNTRY, TWO SYSTEMS

Perhaps Deng's most outstanding pragmatic act was the agreement in September 1984 that Hong Kong should be returned to China in 1997 while retaining its economic and social 'system' for fifty years – 'one country, two systems'. He failed by less than five months to live to see the handover – a dramatic precedent, with implications for the future of Taiwan, which in time was likely to cut into the foundations of the unitary one-party totalitarian state. One guarantee that the separate system for Hong Kong would be maintained was the value of its separate economic system to the rest of China. It seems unlikely that any new leadership will be so unpragmatic as to encourage the hasty breakdown of 'two systems'.

In its last years under the British, Hong Kong had a multiparty Legislative Council in a form which the PRC found unacceptable. It was replaced at midnight on 30 June 1997 by a nominated council with the promise of elections to be held in 1998. By this procedure Martin Lee's Free Democratic party lost power; nevertheless Hong Kong remains another system, politically as well as economically. It is more than likely that before fifty years are up, some political and legal practices from Hong Kong will spread to the rest of China.

10 Chinese society in the 1990s

Visitors to China in the 1990s see signs of dramatic change, particularly in those eastern cities where skyscrapers are mushrooming. However, Chinese society is still faced with some of the old issues; among these are its growing population, and the status of women. There are some new and growing problems – the migration from the countryside to the cities (in 1980 four-fifths of China's population was rural) and the increasing disaffection of the minorities. Among new prospects is the growth of religion and some indication of an emerging civil society.

POPULATION

China's population has been increasing steadily (apart from a slight dip in 1961–2) from 542 million in 1949 to 1,158 million in 1991.[1] Some steps were taken to promote birth control in the mid-1950s. However, during the Great Leap and again during the Cultural Revolution Maoist ideas prevailed over 'bourgeois' Malthusian theory. (Conversely in 1962–66 there was a birth control campaign.) The relatively high birth rate – women in the 1960s often had 5 or 6 children – was offset by the famine in the aftermath of the Great Leap and by poor health in some regions. Campaigns to restrict family size included exhortations against early marriage, but it was not until the 1980s that effective new measures were taken to restrict China's population growth. The one-child family policy combined moral persuasion with material sanctions. Young couples, having been induced to make the pledge, had their names adorned with a ribbon displayed on a notice board. With one child they would be entitled to benefits in housing and education, with two they would lose the benefits and be liable to additional payments e.g. for medical services, for buying grain for the additional child on the free market. In some cases women were coerced into having abortions.[2]

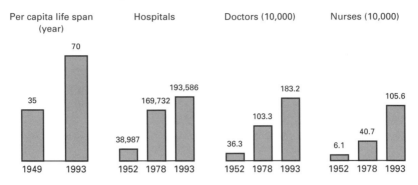

| Per capita life span (year) | Hospitals | Doctors (10,000) | Nurses (10,000) |

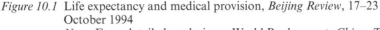

Figure 10.1 Life expectancy and medical provision, *Beijing Review*, 17–23 October 1994
Note: For a detailed analysis see World Bank report, *China, The Health Sector*, Washington D.C., 1984.

Adjusting to the family responsibility system led to serious problems. For country people there was a palpable need for children to work the land and provide for them in their old age. There was also high premium on a son; after all a daughter would leave to join another family. The upshot has been large scale infanticide of baby girls, estimated at 200,000 a year, and, where detected by amniocentesis, the abortion of female foetuses. Sick girl babies have sometimes been left to die. Thus there will be many fewer women than men in China, which is likely to produce a falling birth rate in the long term.

MIGRATION TO THE CITIES

A feature of the Deng era has been the rising tide of migration from the countryside to the cities.[3] City governments have passed new regulations to maintain control and meet the problem of resources caused by the massive drift of 40–50 million people. The authorities have also been faced with the flagrant disregard of family planning laws by the migrant population.

The different manners and cultures of the original urbanites and the rural immigrants have created friction, and open hostility. The country folk have been blamed for rising crime, while they have often seen themselves as victims, exploited by landlords and employers and city slickers in general. There are many real and imaginary grounds for antagonism. It is reported that Beijing office workers prefer not to use the underground now that it means rubbing shoulders with unprepossessing peasants. In many cities the newcomers have been blamed for the disappearance of manhole covers, presumably melted down as scrap metal for a quick yuan. In one year in Beijing alone 200 citizens were injured by falling down open manholes.[4]

The migration has been facilitated by the relaxation of state controls over residence (see Chapter 9). It has been encouraged by the opportunities for higher income in the cities with average per capita urban income approximately three time that in rural areas.

THE CHANGING STATUS OF WOMEN

We have seen (Chapter 1) that the 1950 Marriage Law was a large step towards the emancipation of women. How effectively did this trend continue? How far was the position of women in the PRC determined by the (conscious) policy of party and state; how far was it the (unintended) consequence of other developmental policies?

From 1950 on the social role of women was enhanced by the opportunity for taking a leading role in local community life and by the number who joined the professions, while in all walks of life some women rose to positions of authority. At ground level each team had a women's team leader, with responsibility on the team management committee for women's interests. Those at the very top were there either because they held gender-related posts, e.g. in the Women's Association or were married to political leaders, e.g. Song Qingling, widow of Sun Yat-sen and Wang Guangmei, married to Liu Shaoqui.

In an overview of the Communist period it can be shown that Maoist policies tended to further gender equality while more recent (social) changes have been somewhat retrograde. Advances in the general level of education benefited girls, particularly in the rural areas where traditionally peasants had seen no purpose in educating girls who were going to marry into their husband's family. The figures for 1978 show that 45 per cent of primary school children (in both city and countryside) were girls. In middle schools, 41 per cent were girls, in colleges and universities 24 per cent were women.[5] In the period 1978 to 1994, however, the female population rose by 25 per cent but the number of girls in primary education fell by 9 per cent.

In campaigns of mass participation women sometimes took an enhanced role, or a distinct role outside the family. Thus in the Great Leap Forward they were encouraged to work outside the home. With diversification (in the countryside) women took on new responsibility with new jobs. In the Cultural Revolution, which was spearheaded in

Figure 10.2 'What's wrong with these girls? Surely there are enough clothes
available to cover them?' Cartoonist's comment on westernization,
Beijing Review, 31 January–6 February 1994 (Cartoon, drawn by
Zhao Ren, originally from *Satire and Humor*.)

the universities by female lecturers, female activists shouted no less
loudly than the men.

Women workers in the countryside got on average 80 per cent of the
workpoints allotted to men working in the same teams, either on the
assumption that they were weaker or because the team assessor in the
field, invariably a man, was still prejudiced.

It has been pointed out that women did not have distinct organizations with the initiative to promote their specific interests.[6] They failed to
mount an effective movement against the practice of marrying into other
villages ('patrilocal autonomy'). The male leaders of Mao's revolutionary state saw no reason to promote such a reform[7] – perhaps because it
would have been too socially disruptive – and the practice persists.

The effects of the market economy have been a mixed blessing for
women. On the one hand job opportunities have increased and they
may share with their husbands in choosing how to spend a generally
higher (money) income. Yet some factories may exploit the cheap labour
of young women who leave when they marry. A very high proportion of

the labour force in the special economic zones is made up of migrant workers, predominantly young women.

It was reported in 1996 that 27 out of 42 government organizations admitted to restricting the number of female graduates employed, in open breach of government regulations. With the relaxation of controls, and loose money in the get rich quick ambiance, prostitution and pornography have returned. Violence against women is on the increase: 21 per cent of Beijing husbands confessed to beating their wives (1994 study); two-thirds of the women attempting to drown themselves in Shanghai (1995 study) were battered wives. A measure of China's westernization by 1996 was the setting-up of support services for the female victims of violence.[8]

THE NATIONAL MINORITIES

The population of the 56 defined 'nationalities', the non-Han minority groups, was almost the same in 1990 as in 1950, i.e. about 8 per cent. They occupy about 60 per cent of the area of China. The proportion of non-Chinese in five autonomous regions, Inner Mongolia, Guangxi Zhuang, Tibet, Ningxia, and Xinjiang has not changed greatly except in Xinjiang where Han Chinese immigration reduced the proportion of non-Chinese from 76 per cent in 1948 to 62 per cent in 1992. In border regions certain nationalities have ethnic and cultural ties across the national frontier. The people of Inner Mongolia have kinship with those in the Mongolian Republic. In Xinjiang, Uighurs and Kazakhs have ethnic ties with states of the former Soviet Union. The Muslims in Ningxia feel affinity with Muslims in the Middle East. Tibet has cultural leanings to India and looks for outside support for independence.

The Chinese Communists in granting autonomy to ethnic minorities replaced traditional elites with bureaucratic control and the power of the Party. The Party had a civilizing mission – the 'socialist transformation' – which to the minorities threatened their identity. In the 1950s there were revolts by the Hui people in Ningxia and Qinghai. The peasants of other minorities joined in opposition to co-operativization. There was also an armed rebellion by the Muslims in Gansu and Qinghai in 1958 which was suppressed by the army with a severity which was to be officially regretted in 1980.[9] The period of the Cultural Revolution brought increased repression of the minorities. In the 1970s an effective form of resistance to the Han was the refusal by ethnic party members and cadres to learn the Chinese language or Beijing approved version of native languages as required by central government policy.

Deng's regime sought to placate the nationalities by encouraging cultural autonomy while keeping religion under political control. State funds were available to repair temples, mosques and monasteries. Religious schools re-emerged where for example children learn the Koran. Native languages were tolerated in the media; by 1994 it was claimed that every nationality population of 100,000 or more in Xinjiang had its own radio and television stations.

Deng was hoping that development strategies leading to a higher standard of living would keep the minorities happy. This may well succeed with scattered ethnic groups in the south-western provinces, but it is less likely to placate those peoples with a strong desire for separation, the Uighurs, Mongolians and Tibetans. They are unlikely to be satisfied with anything less than a political solution.

In Xinjiang since 1996 there has been violent direct action by Uighur separatists who, although Muslim, are not fighting an Islamic war but see themselves as resisting the 'imperialism' of Beijing. Their methods include bomb attacks on bridges and arsenals, setting fire to an oil refinery and rioting in at least six towns and cities. It is reported that China now deploys up to one million troops in Xinjiang and Uighur sources report that there were more than 10,000 arrests and 1,000 executions in the first year of disturbances. The troubles continue; in 1997 explosions in Beijing were attributed to Uighur terrorists.[10]

In Chapter 1 we noted the 'liberation' of Tibet, a military move by the 2nd Field Army which was to create considerable tensions. Compared with the other minority regions Tibet was racially homogeneous; the few Han Chinese were almost all imported migrants. The PRC census of 1982 for the Tibetan Autonomous Region recorded a population of 1.9 million with 5 per cent being Han Chinese but it is claimed that there is a total Tibetan population of five or six million, the majority scattered throughout adjoining provinces. The Tibetans are now demanding an end to Chinese immigration; the Dalai Lama's office in exile claimed in 1995 that the Chinese in the Autonomous Region outnumbered the Tibetans by 2.5 to 2 million and by two to one in Lhasa.

The Dalai Lama has lived in exile since his flight to India in 1959. During the Cultural Revolution, which was particularly disastrous for Tibet, the practice of religion was banned from 1966 to 1976 and monasteries were destroyed. Since 1980 when Hu Yaobang made a conciliatory visit to Lhasa, Beijing has given economic benefits such as a tax concession and Tibet has been a major beneficiary of developmental policies. At the same time some critics maintain that Han commercialism is exploiting the Tibetans.[11] The Dalai Lama, who is favoured by Western liberals, advocates the independence of Tibet by peaceful means. In 1989 he was awarded the Nobel Peace prize, but his followers mounted violent demonstrations in Lhasa in 1987, 1988 and 1989 which led to the imposition of martial law for some months. In an attempt to find a compromise, the Dalai Lama proposed that while the Chinese maintain sovereignty and control over foreign policy the Tibetans should be allowed genuine autonomy. The Chinese are adamant that there can be no referendum on Tibet's future. Specifically they rejected a proposal by the International Commission of Jurists for a referendum under UN supervision. 'We perceive the producer of this report as being extremely ignorant of Tibet's history, and extremely ignorant of the principles of international relations and international law'.[12] The Chinese leadership will no doubt continue to uphold the historical claims for Chinese suzerainty and are not unaware of Tibet's mineral resources and its strategic value. Meanwhile the latest invasion of Tibet by consumer goods from China, together with discos, bars and billiards may do more to change the Tibetan perceptions than ever the Communist Party cadres could.

'RELIGION FEVER'

In China today there are an estimated 70 million Buddhists and Daoists, 20 million Muslims and approximately 9 million recognized Christians. We have seen (Chapter 1) that freedom of religious belief – written into the 1954 Constitution – was conditional on breaking ties with foreign churches.

The 4 million Protestants and the 5 million Catholics in the 'three-self' patriotic churches have had a noticeable revival. But there is now an alternative clandestine 'house church movement', the non-denominational Christians, who in spite of – or because of – government crackdowns form vigorous grassroots Christian communities. Although bibles have been printed in Nanjing since 1988, there is, apparently, an insatiable demand which has encouraged bible runners such as the British Squadron Leader Michael Coles who in 1990 ran a hovercraft up the Yangzi, which masquerading as a medical mission, made its main task the supply of bibles to house church groups.[13] Not surprisingly the authorities have reacted with investigations and arrests of the Chinese (not the foreigners) involved. Two decrees were issued in 1994, 'Provisions on the Management of Religious Activities of Foreign Nationals Within the Boundaries of the PRC' and 'Control of Sites of Religious Activities'. By the first, foreigners could visit and worship at approved sites but not seek converts. The second gave legal status to approved meeting places but this was conditional on refraining from 'harmful' activities. Thus there is scope for the authorities to clamp down as in December 1994, when arrests took place all over China.

While the activities of the relatively few Christians have attracted attention in the West, there has been a general upsurge of what has been called 'religion fever'.[14] Buddhism and Daoism are reviving, as well as Islam and Lamaism, which are linked to the national minorities. The state tolerates all these (subject to controls) but does not (theoretically) permit superstitious practices. Popular religion in the countryside, the worship of local deities, has been subject to some surveillance and repression for its superstitious aspects.

Nevertheless, the general spread of superstitious beliefs has not been checked. On the contrary geomancy and fortune telling are regularly practised. There has also been a visible return to such practices as spirit money and the use of firecrackers to exorcise evil spirits. All these changes may be symptomatic of the decline of communist ideology and indicate that there is a void to be filled.

THE PROSPECTS FOR A RESPONSIBLE CIVIL SOCIETY

To what extent has there been some development of popular participation in Chinese politics? The April 1976 demonstrations in Tiananmen Square (see Chapter 8) have been cited as a turning point. Until then manifestations of popular opinion had been orchestrated, in line with the latest mass campaign of the Party.[15] The crowds who insisted on laying wreaths in honour of Zhou Enlai in defiance of officialdom were making a statement against the leadership.

In retrospect the 1976 Tiananmen Incident is seen as the first spontaneous mass protest in the People's Republic and it has been followed by a variety of popular protests, notably the Democracy Wall in 1978–9, student demonstrations in the 1980s and the expressed discontent of workers and peasants in the 1990s.

Since 1989 some sinologists have sought to find an emerging 'civil society' in China. Those who look back to find the origins of a 'public sphere' in traditional China have not reached agreement.[16] Others in their study of mass behaviour from 1989 on became optimistic about the prospects for a civil society.[17] Against this it is argued that the Chinese do not have the concept of civil society sharing power in the state and that mass protests reveal the absence of civil society; for example, student movements tend to be volatile, factional and formless.[18]

It is questionable whether the permitted rise in Deng's later years of small interest groups, such as housing exchange associations and dancing clubs can form the basis of civic pressure groups. They have been described as expressions of *Gemeinschaft*, representing community bonds, rather than of *Gesellschaft* bringing public opinion to bear on the state.[19]

Nevertheless, laws introduced in 1990–1994 may well enhance the prospects for civil society. The Administrative Procedure Law and the State Compensation Law make it possible to sue the government. The Law on Trade Unions and the Arbitration Law could lead to the recognition of citizens rights.[20]

There have been signs of a change in people's attitudes. It is noteworthy that in the official pursuit of culprits after Tiananmen people were reluctant to denounce one another.[21] Since that time too, there have been indications that some people are more willing to express their opinions publicly; in indoctrination sessions certain party leaders have been openly criticized. Perhaps a corner has been turned and the heavy and complete repression of Mao's years has gone for ever.

11 Conclusion

It was said when Deng died in 1997 that his death had already been discounted. The men in place, Jiang Zemin, General Secretary, and Li Peng, Prime Minister, were Deng's appointees. Although they were not young – they were born in 1926 and 1928 respectively – they were a new generation and heading a party and bureaucracy which for two decades had lived with the broad aim of pragmatic modernization. There had been little in the way of political ideology to replace Maoism. The division of opinion had been mainly about the pace and extent of change. Deng had been less equivocal than the conservatives about the importance of the bold way forward – it was the point of his southern journey in 1992. In these terms Deng had remained a revolutionary to the end.

It has been assumed by many commentators that economic change means social change which leads to political change. Regarding the economic change, it is uncontroversial that China is getting richer at an impressive rate. It is clear that this is linked to the open door policies and that the benefits are no longer confined to the special zones (now of less particular consequence) but are seeping inland. It appears, too, that as some get richer others get poorer. Some parts of the country are much better off than others. There is inflation at a rate which was unthinkable two decades ago.

We have seen concomitant social effects beginning in the 1980s which are far from being resolved.

- The local or private control of factories and the free market have meant the end of the 'iron ricebowl' – security – for workers.
- New job opportunities for some have gone hand in hand with unemployment for others.
- Just as power holders have been corruptly using their entrenched positions to get rich, the wheeler-dealing of the free market has spawned fresh corruption.

- The old concept of the welfare of the masses which, in spite of an overall slow growth rate, made China appear an exemplary Third World state has been weakened.
- The Maoist achievement had been to attack the diseases associated with underdevelopment and largely eliminate epidemics by promoting hygiene and health care. In the reform era the diseases of the developed world, heart disease, stroke and digestive diseases are increasing, particularly in the cities, while modern medical facilities are expensive.
- Rapid and uncontrolled industrialization has resulted in serious pollution of the environment. The authorities are well aware of the problem; the matter is raised in the media and even highlighted by cartoons.

THE FIFTEENTH PARTY CONGRESS

The Fifteenth Party Congress in September 1997 was heralded as the occasion for advancing the process of building socialism with Chinese characteristics into the twenty-first century. Its general effect was to confirm the guidelines which were well established at the time of Deng's death. The position of Jiang Zemin as General Secretary was confirmed.

As for ideology, Jiang introduced the term Deng Xiaoping Theory which together with Marxism–Leninism and Mao Zedong Thought constituted a unified scientific system and was accepted by the Party as its guide to action. In short this meant that Deng's policies were to be continued. Stagnating state industries were to be closed down or sold off. The rationale for increasing privatization was that 70 per cent of China's 118,000 state owned industrial concerns were losing money. Jiang noted that this 'strategic readjustment' would cause difficulties for the workforce (it would increase the already large number of unemployed by adding 40 million city workers to the 175 million redundant rural workers looking for jobs). Jiang called for vigilance against the Left, i.e. Maoists opposed to the free market, and warned all workers that they 'should change their ideas about employment and improve their own quality to meet the new requirement of reform and development'.

It remains to be seen how smoothly the on-rolling market can proceed. There are reasons for proceeding cautiously since uncontrolled privatization may well go hand in hand with asset-stripping and corruption. Social discontent may burgeon to the point of explosion.

An important political consequence of corruption is that it is divisive. Local power holders as well as local entrepreneurs both welcome the

Figure 11.1 'Perhaps we ought to get out of his way?' Socialism with Chinese
characteristics as portrayed in the *Beijing Review*, 1–7 January
1990.

decline of the centre. The big question is how long the power of the
Communist Party can survive the relaxation and withering away of the
command economy. How long can the very unity of China survive as
political chiefs and money makers in the provinces thrive in their own
localities? From the beginning the army has been important in holding
the country together. Mao said 'political power grows out of a barrel of
a gun' but he was careful to stress 'the principle is that the Party com-
mands the gun, and the gun must never be allowed to command the
Party'. As the role of the Party at the centre is modified by the great
economic revolution, will it have the same hold over the military chiefs
or is there the possibility that they will develop local allegiances?

Western onlookers see a grand question of democratic rights. It does
not follow that the majority of Chinese are seriously concerned with
this question. Yet, as films, videos and magazines flood freely in, par-

ticularly from countries with Chinese communities, they bring new ideas which must be increasingly difficult to ignore. Such is the spiritual pollution of which the Party leadership warns. The concept of freedom, particularly as a fresh idea, is heady stuff – especially for the young – and appeals to students.

However, in a world in which much lip service is paid to democracy, the Chinese leaders are honest in rejecting what they see as a foreign concept. There are those in the West who agree that China does not need the democratic apparatus of the multiparty state. For example, in a television discussion in 1997 the former British Prime Minister Sir Edward Heath echoed Deng to the effect that 1.2 billion people could not be ruled that way. To which Martin Lee, Chairman, Hong Kong Free Democrats said, 'Why not?' Were the Chinese different from the rest of the world's peoples – that they were unfit to take a genuine responsibility for their own government?

CHINA AND THE WORLD

The Chinese Communists have been in military conflict with seven countries: Japan, the Soviet Union, India, Vietnam, South Korea, Taiwan and the USA. What are the prospects for an era of peace extending into the twenty-first century? The balance of power in the world changed suddenly with the break-up of the Soviet Union which accompanied the fall of communism in that country. Now there is one superpower, the United States of America, to assume with its allies responsibility for world peace, what does the future hold for China?

There is a reassuring prognosis for peace with old enemies. Relations with India are improving. A border agreement was signed with Vietnam in 1996. China looks set to play an increasing role in the economies of the Pacific Rim without alarming its neighbours by excessive domination.[1] But China remains sensitive and has a prima facie case for fearing isolation and encirclement. The security agreement in 1996, signed by President Clinton and Japanese premier Ryutaro Hashimoto, and separate US talks on helping Japan build a missile defence system may well have given Beijing food for thought.

In April 1997 Jiang Zemin visited Moscow to sign the declaration of a 'new bilateral relationship'. The two countries rejected the claims 'by any one country to the role of absolute leader'.[2] It remains to be seen how this will work as a reassertion of a triangular relationship. President Yeltsin said in a hardly veiled reference to President Clinton, 'Someone is longing for a single polar world. He wants to decide things for himself'. The Chinese Xinhua newsagency quoted the declaration: 'No country should seek hegemony, practise power politics or monopolise international affairs.'

The commitment to a multipolar world was reiterated in November 1997 when President Yeltsin met Jiang Zemin in Beijing. Agreements signed by the two leaders included increased bilateral trade, and perhaps most significantly a pact defining the whole course of the 2,800 mile border, which for so long had been bitterly disputed.

However, there is no reason to suppose that the Chinese will sacrifice their rather special relationship with the United States. Most favoured trade status allows the Chinese to profit by their excess of exports over imports with the USA. Conversely, although some American Congressmen may think they can force changes on China, it is questionable how far the USA can push China on human rights. From time to time China responds with a token concession e.g. the most famous dissident, Wei Jingsheng, originally jailed for 15 years in 1979 (see Chapter 8), and who had spent all but a few months since then in prison, was released 'for health reasons' in November 1997.

As they firmly reject the criticism of their regime by parliamentarians in Japan and Taiwan as well as the USA, the Chinese may well feel that any concession on territorial issues, any compromise on 'one China' would threaten their very security. They also seem to fear that concessions on human rights or democratic government will be a wedge breaking the hold of the Communist Party and splitting up the country. This is China's much reiterated position as it enters the twenty-first century. Yet 'one country – two systems' may yet offer a way forward. Could a federal China allowing autonomy in Hong Kong, Taiwan,[3] and Tibet resolve political problems while preserving sovereignty and security? Will alternative political processes from one part of a 'two-systems' China spread to the rest of the country? How long must China remain one great country in which a genuinely elected government is unthinkable?

Notes

Preface

1 H. Kissinger, *The White House Years*, Boston, Little, Brown, 1979, p. 1058.
2 See Paul Hollander, *Political Pilgrims. Travels of Western Intellectuals to the Soviet Union, China and Cuba 1928–1978*, New York, Oxford University Press 1981. Chapter 7.

Introduction

1 Dick Wilson, *Mao the People's Emperor* (London, Hutchinson, 1979), p. 443.
2 See, for example, W. J. F. Jenner, *The Tyranny of History; the Roots of China's Crisis* (London, Allen Lane, Penguin Books, 1992).
3 See, for example, Robert K. G. Temple, *China, Land of Discovery and Invention* (Wellingborough, Patrick Stevens, 1986), which distils Joseph Needham's multi-volume, *Science and Civilization in China*.
4 By the 'unequal' Treaty of Nanjing (1842) foreign nationals enjoyed special privileges, e.g. 'extra-territoriality' – exemption from Chinese laws in the Treaty ports.
5 Robert A. Bickers and Jeffrey N. Wasserstrom, 'Shanghai's "Dogs and Chinese Not Admitted" Sign: Legend, History and Contemporary Symbol', *China Quarterly* no. 142 (June 1995) pp. 444–66. There were *separate* ordinances.
6 Joint Statement, 26 January 1923, *China Year Book*, 1924, p. 863.
7 The details of the negotiations are obscure. Chiang denied that he had made any agreement as a condition of his release.
8 Soviet (Comintern) policy in 1935–6 regarding the united front is disputed by John Garver and Michael Sheng (See *China Quarterly* no. 129 (March 1992) pp. 149–83) Garver argues that Mao was more consistently opposed to Chiang Kai-shek than Stalin who saw the Nationalists as the 'big fish' in China. Sheng does not deny that there were differences of opinion between Mao and Stalin but argues that 'the discrepancies were differences of emphasis, not of substance' (p. 183) and points out that there is no evidence that Stalin asked the CCP to give up its armed forces and territories for the cause of the united front.

9 For example, Edgar Snow, *Red Star over China*, revised and enlarged edition, London, Gollancz, 1968, and Anna Louise Strong, *China Fights for Freedom* (London, Lindsay Drummond, 1939).

10 Of eighteen documents originally selected for study Mao was named as the author of seven and six more carried his views. There were two Soviet documents, by Stalin and one each from Liu Shaoqi, Kang Sheng and Chen Yun. Mark Selden, *The Yenan Way in Revolutionary China* Cambridge, Mass., Harvard University Press, 1971, p. 200.

11 According to Fredrick C. Teiwes and Warren Sun *The Formation of the Maoist Leadership. From the Return of Wang Ming to the Seventh Party Congress*, London, Contemporary China Institute, SOAS Research Notes and Studies, no. 10, 1994. (Reviewed in *China Quarterly* no. 147, September 1996, by Tony Saich) the Comintern's actions and influence worked in Mao's favour.

12 M. Meisner, *Mao's China and After*, London, Macmillan, 1986, p. 43.

13 This has been interpreted, in a later footnote to Mao's selected works as 'a society based on public ownership, free from class exploitation and oppression – a lofty ideal long cherished by the Chinese people. Here the realm of Great Harmony means communist society', *Selected Readings from the Works of Mao Tsetung*, Foreign Languages Press, Beijing, 1971, p. 386.

14 See, for example, Karl A. Wittfogel, 'The Legend of Maoism' Part 1, *China Quarterly*, no. 1, 1960 (January–March) Part 2, ibid., no. 2, 1960 (April–June) and S. Schram, 'Mao Zedong a hundred years on: the Legacy of a Ruler', *China Quarterly* no. 137 (March 1994) pp. 125–43.

15 Chinese scholars called them Mao Zedong sixiang – Mao's thoughts – implying that the suffix -ism (zhuyi) should be kept for systematic doctrines such as Marxism and Leninism.

1 The Communist victory and consolidation of power, 1949–53

1 On 15 August 1945 the Soviet Union signed a Treaty of Friendship and Alliance with the Chinese Nationalist government. This confirmed the agreement made at Yalta in the absence of the Chinese for the restoration of Russian interests in Manchuria and also recognized a separate, i.e. Soviet dominated Outer Mongolia. Henceforth the Soviet Union had a vested interest in the continuation of Chiang Kai-shek's government.

2 J. K. S. Yick *Making Urban Revolution in China. The CCP–GMD Struggle for Beijing–Tianjin*, New York, Sharpe, 1995 examines Mao's strategy for urban insurrection. He argues that the disintegration of the GMD was equally important.

3 These regions evolved from the pattern of communist government in wartime.

4 Jonathan D. Spence *The Search For Modern China*, New York, W. W. Norton, 1990, p. 522

5 All thirteen men held top military party posts, but did not necessarily work in the government.

6 Mao Zedong, 30 June 1949, *On the People's Democratic Dictatorship*.

7 Chiang Kai-shek had envisaged that this bureaucratic capitalism, i.e. control by state (GMD) officials would extend to all private capital. Nigel Harris, *The Mandate of Heaven. Marx and Mao in Modern China*, London, Quartet Books, 1978, p. 39.

8 Spence, op. cit., p. 535. See also S. R. Shalom, *Deaths in China Due to Communism*, Arizona State University, Center for Asian Studies, Occasional Paper no. 15, 1984. He estimates extrapolating from official figures, such as those given for Guangdong, a figure of 1 million for all killings in the first years of communist rule. Others, for example Jacques Guillermaz, diplomat and historian, suggest five million in 1949–52.

9 This figure was disputed. While the Communist Party said that less than one-fifth of the population could read and write, the GMD said the figure was much higher. A. MacKerras and C. Yorke, *The Cambridge Handbook of Contemporary China*, Cambridge, Cambridge University Press, 1991, p. 218. In any case a smaller proportion of women were literate.

10 For example in one of his first articles, 'Miss Chao's Suicide', November 1919.

11 The measures were not entirely new. Not only had there been some emancipation of women residents as well as cadres in Yanan and other communist areas, but the civil code of the nationalist regime introduced in 1930 had in theory anticipated much of the new Marriage Law.

12 Parliamentary Debates 1946–9 vol. 469 col. 2225.

13 Beverley Hooper *China Stands Up, Ending the Western Presence 1948–1950* Allen and Unwin, Sydney, 1986, p. 170.

14 By the mid-1950s all that remained were 'a handful of idealistically committed teachers and translators and involuntary hostages and gaoled missionaries'. Hooper, op. cit., p. 186.

2 'Leaning to one side', 1950–3

1 Allen S. Whiting, *China Crosses the Yalu. The Decision to enter the Korean War*. New York, Macmillan, 1960. This interpretation was based largely on circumstantial evidence because of the difficulty of examining the decision making process in China.

2 Edwin Martin, *Divided Counsel. The Anglo-American Response to Communist Victory in China*. Lexington, University Press of Kentucky, 1986, p. 19

3 Ibid., p. 38

4 While the good faith of the Chinese was widely doubted no one seems to have suspected a hoax. To this day the matter has not been resolved. All of Zhou's aides have denied knowledge of this message (Chen Jian, *China's Road to the Korean War*, New York, Columbia University Press, 1994, p. 241)

5 Dean Acheson, 'Letter of Transmittal', 30 July 1949. *United States Relations with China*. Department of State, Washington D.C., 1949.

6 Sergei Goncharov, John Lewis and Litai Xue, *Uncertain Partners*, Stanford, Stanford University Press, 1993, p. 54.

7 Michael H. Hunt, *The Genesis of Chinese Communist Foreign Policy*, New York, Columbia University Press, 1996, pp. 177–8.

8 Cf. the anti-Tito resolution passed by the Cominform, Goncharov, Lewis and Litai Xue, op. cit., pp. 54–5, and note 309.

9 In spite of Stalin's prevarication Chen Jian believes that a new Sino-Soviet Treaty was 'exactly what Stalin wanted' ('The Sino-Soviet Alliance and China's Entry into the Korean War', Woodrow Wilson International Center for Scholars, Washington D.C., Cold War International History Project Working Paper no. 1, 1992). Paul Wingrove thinks that Stalin was anxious

and hesitant at the prospect of coming to terms with Mao after their 'history of bad relations' ('Mao in Moscow, 1949–50: Some New Archival Evidence' *Journal of Communist Studies and Transition Politics*, vol. 2, no. 4, December 1995).

10 Song Qingling, 'The Difference between Soviet and American Foreign Policies' *People's China*, 16 January 1950, p. 5.

11 Cold War International History Project *Bulletin* no. 6–7 Winter 1995/96, p. 172, col. 3.

12 Secret protocols at Stalin's insistence excluded westerners from taking any part in economic activities in Xinjiang or Manchuria, and provided for the Chinese to sell all their lead, tin and tungsten to the USSR, Wingrove, Ibid.

13 Dick Wilson, *Mao – The People's Emperor*, London, Hutchinson, 1979, p. 267.

14 National Security Council document, April 1950.

15 John Gittings. *The World and China 1922–1972* London, Eyre Methuen, 1974, p. 173.

16 Stalin chose to keep them away so that the Soviet Union could abjure any responsibility. Goncharov, Lewis and Litai Xue, op. cit., p. 161.

17 Ibid., p. 144.

18 Ibid., p. 152. In any case with the focus of Soviet support shifting to Korea the Chinese had to give up ideas of Soviet naval and air support for an attack on Taiwan. The invasion was postponed, first until summer 1951, and then indefinitely.

19 Hua Qingzhao, *From Yalta to Panmunjom*, Ithaca NY, Cornell University Press, 1993, argues that Truman was justified in sending troops to fight in Korea but was wrong to interfere in the Chinese civil war.

20 Chen Jian, *China's Road to the Korean War*, New York, Columbia University Press, 1994, p. 128.

21 Ibid., p. 129.

22 Goncharov, Lewis and Litai Xue, op. cit., p. 181.

23 Harry S. Truman, *Years of Trial and Hope*, London, Hodder and Stoughton, 1956, p. 382.

24 Goncharov, Lewis and Litai Xue, op. cit., p. 190.

25 The question of payment was not raised at the time the arms were sent. All loans were settled by 1965. Ibid., p. 201.

26 Cullum MacDonald, *Korea: The War Before Vietnam*, London, Macmillan, 1986, p. 258.

27 According to US sources the Chinese casualties were 920,000. Chinese sources give a total of 366,000, comprised of 114,000 killed in action, 39,000 other deaths, 21,000 POWs and the rest 'hospitalised' Hua Qingzhao, op. cit., p. 266.

28 Article by Qing Shi, pseudonym of writers at the Central Party History Research Centre, *Hundred Year Tide*, Cited in T. Poole, 'China has second thoughts on Mao's great "triumph"'. The *Independent International*, 6–12 August 1997. Presumably the Chairman was being wise after the event.

3 The politics of the People's Republic, 1953–7

1 R. MacFarquhar, ed. *The Politics of China, 1949–1989*, Cambridge, Cambridge University Press, 1993, p. 51.

2 In 1945 the Seventh Party Congress was held, in 1956 the Eighth, subsequent Congresses were held in 1969, 1973, 1977, 1982, 1987, 1992 and 1997.
3 Mao Zedong, *Selected Works*, vol. V, pp. 173–4.
4 K. Lieberthal, *Governing China From Revolution Through Reform*, New York, Norton, 1995, p. 79.
5 Ibid., p. xv.
6 Article 5, *Sino-Soviet Treaty and Agreements*, F.L.P., Peking, 1950, pp. 5–8.
7 Bo Yibo, *Ruogan Zhongda Juece Yu Shijian De Huigu (A Review of Certain Policies and Events)* vol. 1 Beijing, 1991 reviewed in *China Quarterly*, no. 135 (September 1993), p. 581.
8 MacFarquhar, op. cit., p. 16.
9 D. A. Kaple, *Dream of a Red Factory*, Oxford, Oxford University Press, 1994, see especially pp. viii–ix.
10 In 1980 the charges against Hu Feng were declared groundless. Mao's writings on the affair are in the volume of selected works produced under Hua Guofeng.
11 Zhou Enlai 'On the Question of Intellectuals', 14 January 1956.
12 F. Schurmann, *Ideology and Organization in Communist China*, Berkeley, University of California Press, 1966, p. 132.
13 Its avowed aim was to liquidate those who had come into the ranks of the revolution with suspicious pasts and untold stories.
14 R. MacFarquhar, *Origins of the Cultural Revolution*, vol. 1., London, Oxford University Press, 1974, p. 126.
15 But see S. Karnow, *Mao and China*, New York, Viking, 1972, pp. 88–9. Mao responded to the Hungarian uprising by suggesting that tolerance of intellectuals eroded communist ideology.
16 Wilson, *Mao, The People's Emperor*, London, Hutchinson, 1979, p. 309.
17 Ibid., p. 312.
18 Ibid., p. 314.
19 J. Gray, *Rebellions and Revolutions*, Oxford, Oxford University Press, 1990, pp. 304–5.

4 China's independent road, 1954–64

1 Zhai Qiang, 'China and the Geneva Conference of 1954', *China Quarterly*, no. 129 (March 1992), p. 103.
2 Chen Jian, 'China and the First Indo-China War' *China Quarterly*, no. 133 (March 1993), see esp. pp. 88–9.
3 Zhai, op. cit., p. 105.
4 Ibid., p. 106.
5 Hoang Van Hoan, *A Drop in the Ocean*, Beijing 1987 in Zhai op. cit., p. 104.
6 In September 1953 the Beijing line was that the French must negotiate with the Vietminh. John Gittings, *The World and China 1922–1972*, London, Eyre Methuen, 1974, p. 194.
7 Zhai, op. cit., p. 111.
8 In 1956 when Khrushchev proposed the simultaneous admission of North and South Vietnam as separate states in the United Nations, Ho Chi Minh was reassured by Zhou Enlai that China would not be 'a party to this betrayal'. Han Suyin, *Eldest Son. Zhou Enlai and the Making of Modern China, 1898–1976*, London, Jonathan Cape, 1994, p. 260.

9 Harrison Salisbury, *To Peking and Beyond. A Report on the New Asia*, New York, Quadrangle, 1973, pp. 225–6.
10 Zhai, op. cit., p. 113.
11 5 December 1954. Supplement to *People's China*, 24, 16 December 1954, pp. 6–8.
12 Robert Garson, *The United States and China since 1949*, Madison, Teaneck, Fairleigh Dickinson University Press, 1994, p. 56.
13 R. MacFarquhar, *Sino-American Relations, 1949–71*, Newton Abbot, David and Charles for RIIA, 1972, p. 116.
14 Gittings, *The World and China 1922–1972*, London, Eyre Methuen, 1974, p. 207.
15 Ibid., p. 199.
16 Ibid., pp. 202–3.
17 John Garver, 'New Light on Sino-Soviet Relations, The Memoirs of China's Ambassador to Moscow 1955–62', *China Quarterly*, no. 122, June 1990, p. 305.
18 D. Wilson, *Mao, the People's Emperor*, London, Hutchinson, 1979, p. 338.
19 Ibid., p. 354.
20 Garver, op. cit., p. 304.
21 Jasper Becker, *Hungry Ghosts, China's Secret Famine*, London, John Murray, 1996, p. 247.
22 The disputed territories were the North-East Frontier Agency Region governed by India (successor to the British raj) and the remote Aksai Chin plateau, where in the 1950s the Chinese built a military road (unnoticed by the Indians) linking Tibet and Xinjiang. The discovery of this road in territory claimed by India led eventually to India's decision to mobilize forces to drive the Chinese out of Aksai Chin. The Chinese struck first. In a carefully controlled offensive in October–November 1962 they defeated the Indian forces, re-established the frontier line to the *status quo ante* and unilaterally announced a ceasefire on 21 November.
23 CCP's Proposal Concerning the General Line of the International Communist Movement, 14 June 1963.
24 See M. M. Sheng, 'Response: Mao and Stalin: Adversaries or Comrades?' *China Quarterly*, no. 129 (March 1992), p. 181 in which he disagrees with John Garver's 'traditional' interpretation.
25 Cold War International History Project *Bulletin* nos 6–7, Woodrow Wilson International Center for Scholars, Washington D.C., Winter 1995/96, p. 165.
26 Ibid., p. 149.
27 Garver, op. cit., p. 304.

5 The Great Leap Forward, 1956–64

1 *Socialist Upsurge in China's Countryside* F.L.P Peking 1957, p. 378.
2 Apart from other considerations a policy of self-sufficiency and decentralization in the countryside would undermine the power of the centre. See M. Meisner *Mao's China and After*, New York, The Free Press, 1996, p. 241, the communes 'posed a grave challenge to the functioning of existing party and state bureaucracies,' also William Hinton, *The Great Reversal. The Privatization of China* 1978–1989, New York, Monthly Review Press, 1990,

p. 152, and A. L. Strong, 'Three interviews with Chairman Mao Zedong' *China Quarterly* no. 103 (September 1985), p. 497. 'When I asked (in early March 1959) whether one aim of this (communes) policy was to avoid the creation of a big, centralised, bureaucratic machine, whether in government or industry, Mao replied that this was indeed one of the benefits sought'.

3 The Chinese term *gongshi* applies equally to the Paris commune.

4 Witold Rodzinski, *The People's Republic of China*, London, Collins, 1988, p. 64.

5 Joan Robinson *Notes from China* Oxford, Blackwell, 1964. Considering what had happened in the communes between 1958 and 1963, she gives an enthusiastic picture of the people overcoming the difficulties of the three 'bitter years' of flood and drought.

6 Rodzinski, op. cit., p. 66.

7 William Hinton, *Shenfan*, London, Secker and Warburg, 1983, p. 219.

8 Peng Dehuai (1898–1974) had a distinguished record. He had joined Mao at Jinggangshan in 1928 and played a major part, second only to Zhu De, in early military campaigns, the Long March and in the war against the Japanese. He led an army in the north-west during the civil war. He was commander of the Chinese 'volunteer' forces in Korea and subsequently was appointed Minister of Defence. He had a close relationship with Mao for three decades, with a reputation for being outspoken. It was he who had proposed in 1956 that references to the 'Thought of Chairman Mao' should be removed from the Party constitution.

9 R. MacFarquhar *The Origins of the Cultural Revolution*, vol. II, Oxford, Oxford University Press, 1983, p. 177 .

10 Ibid., p. 200.

11 Ibid., p. 222.

12 D. Wilson, *Mao the People's Emperor*, London, Hutchinson, 1979, p. 352.

13 See Jasper Becker, *Hungry Ghosts*, London, John Murray, 1996, pp. 270–1. In 1993 an article in the Shanghai academic journal *Society*, which was later withdrawn, stated that falsified figures concealed a death toll of forty million.

14 Han Suyin, *Eldest Son. Zhou Enlai and the Making of Modern China, 1898–1976*, London, Jonathan Cape, 1994, p. 275.

15 *Peking Review*, 1 September 1959, p. 14.

16 C. MacKerras and A. Yorke, *Cambridge Handbook of Contemporary China*, p. 22. But cf. Becker op. cit., p. 268 'there was no unusual weather or natural disasters in 1959, 1960 or 1961, and footnote 3, p. 330.

17 Jack Gray, *Rebellions and Revolutions*, Oxford, Oxford University Press 1990, p. 314.

18 Jack Gray, Review of 'China This Century', in *China Quarterly* no. 140 (Dec 1994), p. 1157 and J. Gray, *Rebellions and Revolutions*, p. 316.

19 In support of Mao, Deng Xiaoping criticized 'rightist elements' who refuse to recognize the 'remarkable achievements of the Great Leap Forward . . . they exaggerated the errors that have occurred during the course of the movement, which the masses have corrected. They use these errors as a pretext to attack the Party line'. *People's Daily*, cited in Becker, op. cit., p. 92.

6 The Cultural Revolution, 1965–71

1 R. De Crespigny, *China This Century*, Oxford, Oxford University Press, 1992, p. 231.

2 S. H. and J. M. Potter, *China's Peasants. The anthropology of revolution*, Cambridge, Cambridge University Press, 1990, pp. 80–2.

3 J. Spence, *The Search for Modern China*, New York, W. W. Norton, 1990, p. 596.

4 From the mid-1960s to the early 1970s there was considerable (secret) investment in the central region with Sichuan at its core. Eight provinces with 38 per cent of China's total population had 53 per cent of total national investment in 1966–70. By comparison their share in 1985 was 24.6 per cent. See T. Cannon, and A. Jenkins, *The Geography of Contemporary China*, London, Routledge, 1990, pp. 36–9.

5 Jiang Qing, a young actress from Shanghai, went to Yanan in 1937. She met Mao and with the reluctant approval of Party leaders married him in 1939. (Mao had previously been married three times: (1) by arrangement, to a village girl when he was 13; (2) to his first love Yang Kaiwei killed by the Nationalists in 1930; and (3) to He Zizhen who accompanied Mao on the Long March, was wounded, and eventually went to Moscow for treatment.) As Mao's wife, Jiang Qing did some secretarial work but did not become prominent until the Cultural Revolution when she led the attack on 'bourgeois' literature and art.

6 Did Mao seriously object to the play as an attack on himself? It is suggested Mao may well have encouraged Wu Han to write the play. R. MacFarquhar (ed.), *The Politics of China, 1949–1989*, Cambridge, Cambridge University Press, 1993, p. 166. See B. Barnouin and Changgen, *Ten Years of Turbulence*, London, Kegan Paul, 1993, p. 17 and footnote p. 304. Before the play was condemned by the media in 1966 most people had not regarded it as a covert attack on Mao.

7 Dick Wilson, *Mao The People's Emperor*, London, Hutchinson, p. 390.

8 Hongqi (Red Flag), 19 October 1980 for events at Beijing university cited in R. MacFarquhar (ed.), *The Politics of China 1949–1989*, Cambridge, Cambridge University Press, 1993, p. 173.

9 *China Pictorial*, 1966, no. 10, p. 4.

10 J. Gray *Rebellions and Revolutions*, Oxford, Oxford University Press, 1990, p. 344.

11 K. H. Fan, *The Chinese Cultural Revolution*, New York, Monthly Review Press, 1968, p. 163.

12 Wilson, op. cit., p. 401.

13 Lowell Dittmar, *Current Scene* 11, no. 1, 1973 1–13, 'The Cultural Revolution and Fall of Liu Shaoqi' suggests Mao was still prepared to work with Liu, but this is a contested point.

14 Wilson, op. cit., pp. 404–5.

15 Named after the Paris Commune of 1871. In February 1966 an article in *Hongqi* had recommended it as the model for government in which officials should be elected and paid the same as ordinary workers.

16 S. Schram, *Chairman Mao Talks to the People: Talks and Letters 1956 – 1977*, New York, Pantheon, 1974, p. 277.

17 Chen Boda, Jiang Qing, Chang Chunqiao and others. They had been supported by Lin Biao and for most of the time by Zhou Enlai.

18 Wilson, op. cit., p. 412.
19 Changes took place earlier, i.e. in the 23 articles (1965) it was stipulated that the basic unit was the brigade; later, the team took over.
20 Jack Gray, op. cit., p. 366 says this was 'by far the most significant gain for the forces of the Cultural Revolution.'
21 Wilson, op. cit., p. 421.
22 Because Zhang was associated with the Gang of Four he was denounced in the aftermath of their fall. He was imprisoned for counter-revolutionary activities in 1983.
23 Educational and social fashion in the West in the 1960s and after which coincidentally took on Maoist aspects did not renege on the experience. For example, it has taken very much longer for elitist education based on selection by exams to replace the democratic coursework approach of the comprehensive.
24 Chen Boda. Born of a peasant family in Fujian he joined the Party during the time of the first united front. After the attack on the Communists in 1927, he spent some time in Moscow. He went to Yanan in 1937 soon became Mao's secretary and was recognized as a top theoretician. Later he became deputy director of the Party's propaganda department and had a part in editing Mao's *Collected Works*. From 1966 he was a member of the Cultural Revolution Group supporting Mao.
25 Philip Bridgeman, 'The Fall of Lin Piao', *China Quarterly* no. 55 (July 1973) p. 435.
26 Harrison Salisbury, *The New Emperors, Mao and Deng: A Dual Biography*, London, Harper Collins, 1992, p. 286 suggests Lin Biao's addiction to morphine may have induced delusions.
27 Yao Ming-le, *The conspiracy and murder of Mao's heir*, London, Collins 1983.
28 MacFarquhar, op. cit., p. 244.
29 K. S. Karol, *The Second Chinese Revolution*, New York, Hill and Wang, 1974. William Hinton, *Turning Point in China*, New York, Monthly Review Press, 1972, described it as 'a class struggle' . . . to determine whether China will continue to take the socialist road and carry the socialist revolution through to the end.
30 K. Mehnert, *Peking and the New Left: At Home and Abroad*, Berkeley, University of California, 1969. Discussed in Lynn T. White, *Politics of Chaos*, Princeton, Princeton University Press, 1989, p. 28.
31 The state support for hierarchy in local units had 'forced people into clientage more surely than the feudal legacy of Confucian patriarchy ever did.' White, op. cit., p. 8.
32 Stanley Rosen, *Red Guard Factionalism and the Cultural Revolution in Guangzhou*, Westview, Boulder, Colorado, 1982, argues that class origin does partly explain the factional participation by university students but not students in secondary schools. Nor was it the key determinant for university students (pp. 5–6). The crucial factor was the 'ideological acceptance of Maoism'.

7 A Great Power Triangle, 1964–79

1 'Why Khrushchev Fell', *Red Flag*, 21 November 1964, Peking Review, 7, 48, 28 November 1964, pp. 6–9.

2 We now know that the Americans manufactured that excuse for intervention, to railroad Congress and used it to justify the massive aerial
bombardment of North Vietnam in spring 1965.
3 Golam Choudhury, *China in World Affairs. The Foreign Policy of PRC
Since 1970*, Epping, Bowker, 1982, p. 40.
4 Ibid., p.42. See also, *Military Balance 1969*, London, Institute of Strategic
Studies, 1970.
5 R. K. I. Quested, *Sino-Russian Relations*, Sydney, George Allen & Unwin,
1984, p. 139.
6 John Garver, *China's Decision for Rapprochment with the United States*,
Boulder, Colorado, Westview Press, 1982, p. 156. Also Frederick C. Teiwes
and Warren Sun, *The Tragedy of Lin Biao. Riding the Tiger during the
Cultural Revolution 1966–1971*, London, Hurst and Co., 1996, p. 125 footnote.
7 For example, R. K. I. Quested, op. cit., p. 141.
8 Zhou Enlai said the accusation was 'nonsense and an insult to the Party'
King C. Chen, ed., *China and the Three Worlds*, Ann Arbor, Michigan,
M. E. Sharpe, 1979, p. 138.
9 See F. C. Teiwes and Warren Sun, op. cit., pp. 124–6.
10 Richard M. Nixon, *Memoirs*, London, Sidgwick & Jackson, 1978, p. 545.
11 On 18 December Mao in an interview with his old friend Edgar Snow said,
'at present the problems between China and the USA would have to be
solved with Nixon', and he would be happy to talk with him either as tourist
or President. On the same visit Snow was enigmatically told by a senior
Chinese diplomat, 'Nixon is getting out of Vietnam', Nixon, op. cit., p. 54.
12 Henry Kissinger, *The White House Years*, London, Weidenfeld & Nicolson,
1979, p. 720.
13 Ibid., p. 748.
14 The informality of the journey is highlighted by the fact that having packed
no shirts he had to borrow one several sizes too big.
15 A US sponsored motion which would have permitted the Republic of China
(Taiwan) to keep its seat was defeated by 59 to 55 with 15 abstentions.
16 Joint Communiqué agreed by the Chinese and US sides in Shanghai, 27
February 1972.
17 Chen, op. cit., p. 138.
18 Kissinger, op. cit., p. 1062.
19 Nixon later said this had been the subject of tough negotiation.
20 Kissinger, *Years of Upheaval*, Boston, Little Brown, 1982, p. 67 and p. 69.

8 A decade of transition, 1972–81

1 The fifth member, Kang Sheng, was mortally ill.
2 R. M. Field, 'The Performance of Industry During the Cultural
Revolution: Second Thoughts', *China Quarterly* no. 108 (Dec 1986), p. 627.
3 R. MacFarquhar, *The Politics of China, 1949–1989*, Cambridge, Cambridge
University Press, 1993, p. 296.
4 D. Wilson, *Mao, The People's Emperor*, London, Hutchinson, 1979, pp.
441–2.
5 On 8 April the *People's Daily* announced that henceforth he would be premier in his own right.

6 The term had been used as early as 1973 when Mao warned against forming a 'Gang of Four' but came into general use after Mao's death.
7 Wang Dongxing was 17 years old when he joined the Jiangxi Soviet in 1933, he served as Mao's bodyguard during the Long March and at Yanan. After Liberation he developed the force known as Unit 8341 which had the responsibility for protecting Party leaders. During the Cultural Revolution this unit presided over the arrests of Peng Zhen, Liu Shaoqi and Deng Xiaoping. It was said that it had protected Mao against the alleged coup of Lin Biao.
8 MacFarquhar, op. cit., p. 314.
9 When Deng was asked what he meant by the phrase he said: 1. He couldn't remember; 2. Whatever it was, it referred to the time he said it.
10 D. Goodman, *Beijing Street Voices*, London, Boyars, 1981, pp. 79, 95.
11 The son of a keen Maoist cadre he was active in the Cultural Revolution. He trained as an electrician and served for four years in the PLA. In 1979 Wei was jailed for fifteen years for giving state secrets to foreigners. He was released six months early in 1993 and continued to criticize the government's record on human rights. He went back to prison.
12 Wei Jingsheng, *The Courage to Stand Alone*, New York, Viking, 1997.
13 *A Great Trial in Chinese History*, Beijing, New World Press, 1981, p. 1.
14 Ibid., p. 3.
15 Chen Boda was accused of collaborating with Lin Biao and Jiang Qing in their efforts 'to seize supreme power'. He was said to have controlled the mass media for counter-revolutionary purposes, and to have been a leader of the attack on Liu Shaoqi. See *A Great Trial in Chinese History*, p. 226.
16 *A Great Trial in Chinese History*, p. 10.
17 For discussion of the resolution see R. Baum, *Burying Mao*, Princeton, Princeton University Press, 1994, pp. 136–7 and p. 42 footnote 90.
18 Hua retained the ceremonial post of Party Chairman temporarily. When the Twelfth Party Congress met in September 1982 it adopted a new Party Constitution which did away with the position of Party Chairman. The highest post, that of Party Secretary, went to Hu Yaobang.
19 Ye Jianying, Li Xiannian, Chen Yun, Deng Xiaoping.
20 Central Document no. 23 (1981) In *Inside China Mainland* 3 12 (December 1981):1, cited in Baum, op. cit., p. 134.

9 'Socialism with Chinese characteristics', 1981–9

1 *Beijing Review* 27, 29 July 1984: 30 cited in R. Baum, *Burying Mao*, Princeton, Princeton University Press, 1994, p. 169.
2 R. De Crespigny, *China This Century*, Oxford, Oxford University Press, 1992, pp. 290–2.
3 It was created a province separate from Guangdong in 1988.
4 See, for example, 'Hu Qiaomu Warns in Xiamen that Foreign investment Enterprises are not concessions', Ming Bao, translated in Foreign Broadcast Information Service, 24 June 1985.
5 His misdemeanour had been to get funds from the mainland which made him a local hero. His special talents were recognized by Beijing three years later when he was made deputy mayor of Guangzhou; further promotion followed.
6 J. Gittings, *Real China, From Cannibalism to Karaoke*, London, Simon & Schuster, 1996, p. 243.

7 William Hinton, *The Great Reversal. The Privatization of China*, New York, Monthly Review Press, 1990.

8 See for example Sybille van der Sprenkel, 'The Chinese Experience of Law – A Historical Survey', *Poly Law Review*, vol. 16, no. 1, Autumn 1980, pp. 5–8. For discussion of the legal profession in China see W. E. Butler, 'Legal Education and the Legal Profession in China', *Poly Law Review*, vol. 16, no. 1, Autumn 1980, pp. 21–26, Butler contrasts legal developments in China with the USSR and Mongolia.

9 Previously foreign traders, notably the 48 Group of British entrepreneurs, had relied on a system of bartering also known as 'compensation trade', See P. Timberlake, *The Ice Breakers*, London, 48 Group, 1994.

10 International Monetary Fund, 17 April 1980; World Bank, 15 May 1980.

11 *Cambridge History of China*, vol. 15, Cambridge, Cambridge University Press, 1991, p. 400.

12 K. Lieberthal, *Governing China*, New York, Norton, 1995, p. 436.

13 J. Gray, *Rebellions and Revolutions*, Oxford, Oxford University Press, 1990, p. 410.

14 Brantly Womack, ed. *Contemporary Chinese Politics in Historical Perspective*, Cambridge, Cambridge University Press 1991, p. 34.

15 Entered Beijing university to read astrophysics aged 16, expelled from Party in anti-rightist campaign of 1957, rehabilitated in the late 1970s and became Vice-President of the University of Science and Technology.

16 Xinhua, 28 December 1986, Foreign Broadcast Information Service, 30 December 1986, pp. K6–K8 in Brantly Womack, op. cit., p. 40.

17 The pattern of *fang* (relaxation) and *shou* (control) appeared as successive periods of economical/political liberalization followed by conservative reaction. R. Baum, 'The Road to Tiananmen: Chinese Politics in the 1980s' in R. MacFarquhar, (ed.) *The Politics of China 1949–1989*, Cambridge, Cambridge University Press, 1993, p. 341 note.

18 CLG 21.1 Spring 1988, 18–21, cited in MacFarquhar, op. cit., pp. 398–9.

19 MacFarquhar, op. cit., pp. 400–1.

20 Li Xiannian had been appointed in 1983. The Sixth NPC had resurrected the post of President/Head of State which had been abolished in the first sessions of Fourth 1975 and Fifth 1978 NPC in line with Mao's thinking. MacFarquhar, op. cit., p. 477

21 Han Minzhu, *Cries for democracy: Writings and Speeches from the 1989 Chinese Democracy Movement*, Princeton, Princeton University Press 1990, pp. 84–5.

22 Los Angeles Times 25 June 1989 in C. Dietrich, *People's China*, Oxford, Oxford University Press, 1994, p. 292.

23 Suggestions to account for this manoeuvre are: 1. It was to be the pretext for a serious crackdown 2. The soldiers were to be given weapons in the square sent separately on buses, but the buses were held up. See MacFarquhar, op. cit., p. 457.

24 MacFarquhar, op. cit., p. 456 gives sources for these figures in footnote.

25 Michel Oksenberg, *et al.*, (eds), *Beijing Spring, 1989: confrontation and conflict: the basic documents*, Armonk NY, M. E. Sharpe, 1990, pp. 376–82.

26 *Guardian*, 10 June 1989, p. 1

10 Chinese society in the 1990s

1 Overall increases in food production since 1949 averaging 3–4 per cent, even before the agricultural reforms of the 1980s, were negated by the rise in population. The per capita food supply in 1978 was no higher than in 1957. J. Gray, *Rebellions and Revolutions*, p. 387.
2 For penalties see Steven Mosher, *The Broken Earth, The Rural Chinese*, New York, Free Press, 1983, Chapter 9.
3 The new definition of urban areas has included farmers working in the outskirts, so figures for population in the expanded cities include many who are not industrial workers.
4 M. Blecher, *China Against the Tides*, p. 159, *Jingji ribao* 13 September 1995.
5 Blecher, op. cit., pp. 153–4.
6 Ibid., p. 156.
7 D. Davin, *Women – Work and the Party in Revolutionary China*, Oxford, Clarendon, 1976, argues feminist issues were soft-pedalled so as not to confuse class issues.
8 Blecher, op. cit., p. 157.
9 A. P. L. Liu, *Mass Politics in the People's Republic*, Boulder, Colorado, Westview Press, 1996, p. 202.
10 *Economist*, 23 August 1997, p. 19.
11 D. Wilson, *China The Big Tiger*, London, Little, Brown & Co., 1996, pp. 310–11.
12 *Guardian*, 24 December 1997, p. 9.
13 R. Barnett, *China Now*, no. 137, 1991, p. 9.
14 J. Gittings, *Real China. From Cannibalism to Karaoke*, London, Simon & Schuster 1996. Chapter 3. See also Bob Whyte, *Unfinished Encounter*, London, Collins, 1988. Kim Kwongchan and Alan Hunt, *Prayers and Thoughts of Chinese Christians*, London, Mowbray, 1991.
15 But see J. Gittings, *China Changes Face*, pp. 152–3, for the revival of manifestos and poems from the Cultural Revolution.
16 See *Modern China*, vol. 19, no. 32, April 1993.
17 See J. N. Wasserstrom and Elizabeth Perry, (eds) *Popular Protest and Political Culture in Modern China, Learning from 1989*, Boulder, Colorado, Westview Press, 1992. A chapter by Perry notes the importance of independent entrepreneurs in democratic politics and the support some gave to students in Shanghai and Beijing in 1989.
18 Liu, op. cit., p. 227.
19 Liu, op. cit., p. 226.
20 See L. Pye, 'The State and the Individual: An Overview Interpretation', *China Quarterly* no. 127, (September 1991).
21 Jung Chang, *China Now*, no. 140, 1992, p. 23.

11 Conclusion

1 At least not in the short term. See for example Stuart Harris and Gary Klintworth, *China as a Great Power. Myths, Realities and Challenges in the Asia–Pacific Region*, New York, St. Martin's Press, 1995, p. 361.
2 *Guardian*, 23 April 1997.
3 The concept of two Chinas is no longer unthinkable in Taiwan. In an interview in November 1997 President Lee of the Republic of China said that

China was essentially a 'culture' not necessarily one country. Until the People's Republic became a free, democratic, socially just country, unification was not possible. However, he did not rule out a federal solution. *The Times*, 10 November 1997.

Further reading

Baum, Richard, *Burying Mao. Chinese Politics in the Age of Deng Xiaoping*, Princeton, Princeton University Press, 1994.

Benewick, Robert and Wingrove, Paul (eds), *China in the 1990s*, London, Macmillan, 1995.

Cambridge History of China, vol. 14, (Roderick MacFarquhar and J. K. Fairbanks (eds)), *The People's Republic*, part 1, 1945–1965, Cambridge University Press, 1987.

Cambridge History of China, vol. 15, *The People's Republic*, part 2, Cambridge University Press, 1991.

Gittings, John, *China Changes Face. The Road from Revolution, 1949–1989*, Oxford, Oxford University Press, 1989.

Goodman, David, *Deng Xiaoping and the Chinese Revolution*, London, Routledge, 1994.

Hinton, Harold, ed., *The People's Republic of China, A Documentary Survey*, 5 vols, Wilmington, Scholarly Resources, 1980.

Hinton, William, *Fanshen. A Documentary of Revolution in a Chinese Village*, New York, Monthly Review, 1966.

——, *Shenfan*, London, Secker and Warburg, 1983.

Hua Qingzhao, *From Yalta to Panmunjom*, Ithaca NY, Cornell University, 1993.

Li Xiao Jun, *The Long March to the Fourth of June*, London, Duckworth, 1989.

Lieberthal, Kenneth, *Governing China. From Revolution Through Reform*, New York, W. W. Norton, 1995.

MacFarquhar, R., *The Origins of the Cultural Revolution 1. Contradictions Among the People 1956–1957*, London, Oxford University Press, 1974.

——, *The Origins of the Cultural Revolution 2. The Great Leap Forward 1958–1960*, New York, Columbia University Press, 1983.

——, *The Origins of the Cultural Revolution 3. The Coming of the Cataclysm 1961–1966*, London, Oxford University Press and Royal Institute of International Affairs, 1997.

Meisner, Maurice, *Mao's China and After*, New York, The Free Press, 1986.

Nathan, Andrew J. and Ross, Robert S., *The Great Wall and the Empty Frontiers. China's Search for Security*, New York, W. W. Norton, 1997.

Salisbury, Harrison E., *The New Emperors. Mao and Deng: A Dual Biography*, London, HarperCollins, 1992.

Schram, Stuart, *The Political Thought of Mao Tse-tung*, New York, Praeger, 1969.

——, *Mao Zedong. A Preliminary Re-assessment*, New York, St Martin's Press, 1984.

Schurmann, Franz, *Ideology and Organization in Communist China*, Berkeley, University of California, 1966.

Selden, Mark, *The People's Republic of China. A Documentary History of Revolutionary Change*, New York, Monthly Review Press, 1979.

Sewell, William, *I Stayed in China*, London, Allen and Unwin, 1966.

Spence, Jonathan, *The Search for Modern China*, New York, W. W. Norton, 1990.

White, L. III, *Policies of Chaos. The Organizational Causes of Violence in China's Cultural Revolution*, Princeton, Princeton University Press, 1989.

Wilson, Dick, *Mao. The People's Emperor*, London, Hutchinson, 1979.

Witke, Roxane, *Comrade Chiang Ch'ing*, Boston, Little Brown, 1977.

Zhisui Li, *The Private Life of Chairman Mao. The Memoirs of Mao's Personal Physician*, Chatto and Windus, 1994.

Index